I0901742

RESTORING THE EARTH

A TESTIMONY OF HOPE FOR GOD'S CREATION

OWEN D. OWENS

Judson Press™
DISTINGUISHED PUBLISHERS SINCE 1824
VALLEY FORGE, PA

Restoring the Earth: A Testimony of Hope for God's Creation

Interior design by Hampton Design Group.
Cover design by Anthony Aranha.

Library of Congress Cataloging-in-Publication data
Library of Congress Control Number: 2025945054

Printed in the U.S.A.
First printing, 2025.

CONTENTS

Editor's Note

Rachael B. Lawrence, Associate Publisher, Judson Press

We at Judson Press first became acquainted with Owen Owens during Advent 2023. Our colleague Vincent Dent at the American Baptist Home Mission Societies recorded an interview with Owen, which he shared at our company All-Staff Gathering in early December. Around the same time, my mentor in ministry, Thomas Carr, contacted me, urging us at Judson to consider publishing Owen's book, a sentiment Vince echoed. Their requests bore urgency, for they knew their longtime friend had terminal pancreatic cancer and limited time remaining. They were eager to share Owen's collected reflections on the environment through a theological perspective, as Owen was an early thought-leader in the field of ecotheology and racial justice for ABCUSA. As his obituary states, "Owen was an untiring champion for the environment and social justice, having contributed to community and environmental groups too numerous to name. For fifty years, he sought to 'learn how God is leading us to a future of ecological wholeness and social justice, where the Biblical hope of peace on earth becomes daily reality.'"[1]

One December day, our publisher, Cheryl Price, and I drove to meet Owen in person. Vince joined us, as they were longtime friends, and American Baptist Home Mission Societies (then called National Ministries of American Baptist Churches USA) had earlier employed Owen. As we visited with him, Owen shared his vision for this book and his excitement for sharing many of the insights God blessed him with during his years in research and ministry, traveling across the United States to witness our changing environment and to seek faithful solutions to help. He told us many of the stories shared in this book, recounting his trip to see the mountaintop removal mining in West Virginia, talking about how caring for the environment is also caring for ourselves, and discussing his ongoing peace-seeking with his cancer. At the end of the conversation, he told me, "It [the book] is almost complete, but friends have told me I need an editor. I won't be here to work with you on the book, but I trust you."

Owen ministered to people every day he could, and I believe he wanted to publish this work as a way to continue his ministry. His strong pastoral presence became clear in our meeting, as his long-time friend Vince was overcome with emotion. Owen gently comforted Vince, reminding him that he would be meeting our Creator and would soon be at peace. He acknowledged the realness of loss for the people he would be leaving behind, while communicating clearly that his hope remained in the Lord who made heaven and earth.

In turn, our hope at Judson Press is to minister to Owen by helping refine this work so he can continue to preach words of hope in a hurting world although absent from the earth and rejoicing with his Creator. We are grateful to Tom Carr, who let us borrow Owen's notes on ecotheology for a while so we could verify some of his sources and remain true to his voice. While this work has been edited, we sought to preserve as much of the original language as possible while clarifying the flow.

The working title of this book was *Rescue the Perishing: Restore the Earth and Ourselves*. The inspiration was from an old hymn, penned by Fanny Crosby in 1869. The first verse sang:

> Rescue the perishing; care for the dying;
> Snatch them in pity from sin and the grave.
> Weep o'er the erring one; lift up the fallen;

Tell them of Jesus, the Mighty to Save.
Rescue the perishing; care for the dying.
Jesus is merciful; Jesus will save.[2]

This hymn inspired Owen as he reflected on the challenges of rescuing others while searching for healing and hope during illness. While we have adjusted the title to reflect what we believe describes the content, we have retained these ideas by dividing the work into two sections. The first section, "Rescue the Perishing," contains reflections from Owen's time witnessing environmental destruction and ideating ways of healing creation. The second section, "Restore the Earth and Ourselves," contains essays focused on making peace with issues of life and death. The book opens with Owen's "Hopeful Prologue," which reminds us to hold on to hope amid the darkness, whether we are facing existential threats of a personal nature or at the global level. God is with us through it all.

Being entrusted with the words of one who has gone to his reward is a blessing. We are grateful for Owen's life and ministry, and we hope that this book supports you in your sojourn in seeking a just and whole world and a peaceful life.

Notes

1. Owen Dale Owens Obituary, Founds-Feryos Cremation and Burial Service, LLC, June 16, 2025, https://www.foundsferyo.com/obituaries/Owen-Dale-Owens?obId=30488480.

2. Fanny J. Crosby, "Rescue the Perishing" (1869, public domain).

Hopeful Prologue

What can we hold on to in fearful times? Disease, death, famine, war—the four horsemen of the apocalypse—are loose. "Do not fear, for I am with you; do not be afraid, for I am your God; I will strengthen you; I will help you; I will uphold you with my victorious right hand," says the One who made us (Isaiah 41:10). "Turn to me and be saved" (Isaiah 45:22). God has urged people through the ages to hold on to the hope of God's promises.

"Oh, come on now," I hear you saying. "You're a minister—that's what I'd expect to hear from you. What's the hook? And how can I hold on to someone or something I can't see or touch?" Well, there is a hook, but not one that you're caught on to be eaten. When you lean on the Holy One and let the warm, loving light of God shine on you, you begin to shine in kindly, powerful ways. Feeling and sharing the love of God can get you in trouble, for those who are led to serve the Lord of heaven and earth meet determined opposition. The Lord of all promises full spiritual might as we follow the Spirit's leading to ecological wholeness and social justice—and ultimately, peace on earth.

In every generation, the Spirit of the living God has transformed darkened minds to shining lights. Since the resurrection of Christ, people have preached the good news of the loving God revealed in Jesus Christ—on the frontier, in foreign lands, and in the growing cities. Those who heard and accepted Christ as their Lord and Savior were baptized, and new churches were started. In American history, mission societies supported this work as the United States expanded westward, funding and supplying missionaries. Because of this work, adults joined together in Sunday schools, class meetings, Bible studies, and prayer groups to learn and practice Jesus' teachings. Believers joined together to organize Christian colleges and seminaries not only to educate believers but also to prepare the next generation of preachers, missionaries, doctors, nurses, and teachers. Voluntary associations came together to restore the United States of America to its God-inspired purpose to be a haven of peace on earth with liberty and justice for all—abolishing slavery, supporting women's right to vote, conserving nature, forming settlement houses, seeking world peace, and reforming government and other institutions.

Throughout my life, I have witnessed God's redemption of human beings who give themselves to shape a new creation. We must remember that the healing of this hurting world is possible. Faith leaders in this precarious time are called to do such things as these:

- Turn from the broad road toward an abyss onto the narrow one that leads to life.
- Preach the good news that God's kingdom is right here—in and around us—and that the Lord provides and guides.
- Form caring and inclusive congregations with people who turn to the way of life.
- Teach life seekers to love God, neighbor, and themselves and to do all the Lord has commanded, restoring nature and regenerating human communities.
- Form and support ecology-justice associations seeking to change institutions and nations for the better.

"Owen, my congregation and community are divided," I hear you say. "If I'm honest and preach the good news of God's kingdom on earth, will I be asked to leave my church?" Many people are unprepared to hear that God intends for them to live in ways that support a healthy ecology. We cannot retreat from that truth. If the bugle gives an uncertain sound, who will prepare for the battle? If we Christians, for instance, don't proclaim Christ's life-saving power and teach God's commandments to love our Lord and our neighbor as ourselves, who is going to do it?

The way we best prepare for hurricanes illustrates how the light of life calls us as agents of blessing in troubled times. Ministers, priests, rabbis, and imams share messages like, "No matter how dark the clouds loom, hope in the Lord and love your neighbor as yourself." Scientists study weather patterns to predict what is likely to happen. Political, business, National Guard, community, and religious leaders of all faiths work together to prepare for storms. Radio and television present information essential to survival, and for a while, commercials and words of anger and hate almost disappear from public discourse. Almost everybody realizes that the good of each and all go together, and many go out of their way to help those without physical strength or money.

"And remember, I am with you always, to the end of the age," said the Lord (Matthew 28:20). I invite you to remember the words of Jesus as you read this book. I remind us that during a time of climate change, we are called to turn to the Lord and live, inspired by the life-saving and peaceful power of Jesus Christ. Light shines, even in southern West Virginia, where mountaintop removal leaves the land looking like the surface of the moon. Love lights the way through suffering and death when we decide to love God and neighbor and live in loving ways. As we study and learn, the light of truth illuminates ways forward through the painful predicaments that generations of human decisions have created.

In times of testing, a rescuing God reaches out to us, calling us to rescue the perishing and become *anthropos anglers* (fishers of people). When we humans decide to turn to God, the Lord's grace, mercy, and love surround us, like babies in our mothers' arms. Through God's atoning grace, we are restored to being truly human beings, and our Savior walks with us as we resume our task of tilling and keeping the garden. The Lord regenerates persons, families, congregations, and voluntary associations to be agents of refuge and mission. He also provides us with creative ways to restore the earth and to invest in the kind of future God wants us to live into.

Adversity met with the will to use money, power, and position for the common good—not for individual gain—creates an enduring community, a commonwealth, and peace on earth. Light shines around you. Decide to enter the light. You'll see.

Section 1
Rescue the Perishing

CHAPTER 1

Light Shines from Coal Country

An Angler Reflects

As I get older, the eyes of trout flies seem to get smaller. When I try to get the leader through the eye of a fly, I fail until I hold the fly where the light illuminates the tiny hole—then the insertion is easier. When a big storm comes at night and the power fails, suddenly all is dark. We can't see anything. Fumbling around, we look for matches and a candle, find them, light the candle, and suddenly the whole room is illuminated.

According to Jesus and the Jewish prophets who went before him, people are created to shine with the compassionate, truthful light of God's steadfast covenant love (the Hebrew word *hesed*, meaning loving-kindness). When we open ourselves to the Lord, warm healing light illuminates our minds and hearts. Then we acknowledge our faults and failures and begin to see clearly the changes we must make to cease to do evil and learn to do good (Isaiah 1:16-17). After teaching the Beatitudes to his disciples, Jesus said, "You are the light of the world. A city built on a hill cannot be hid" (Matthew 5:14).

Blood on the Mountains

In March 2010, my friend David Dunbar, head of the biology department of Cabrini College, called me. "Owen," he said, "Larry Gibson is going to speak to our students and faculty. Come over and hear what he has to say." So I did. The room was full. Larry entered wearing a neon green T-shirt. I remembered meeting him at a Washington, DC, meeting of the National Religious Coalition for Creation Care. I sat and listened to his message.[1]

Larry said that when he returned to West Virginia in the 1990s, he saw a method of coal mining that involved blasting mountains apart to extract coal and then shoving the rubble into adjacent valleys. Companies were mechanizing, providing fewer and fewer jobs, and the huge draglines, dynamite, and bulldozers left devastation behind them. Communities were unsafe to live in. Many suffered from cancer and lung disease as silicon dust and toxic residues of the dynamite used to blow up the mountains poisoned the air and water. Ecosystems were being torn to pieces.

"What can I do to save this land I love?" Larry wondered. He sought to understand what was happening in West Virginia and talked to leaders who had given their lives seeking justice. When the coal mining company offered him big money to buy his family's ancestral land on Kayford Mountain, Larry refused. "I don't want to sell myself, my culture, my people for anything!" Soon silicone dust clouded the sky. Right to the edge of his land came the explosions. Multiton boulders crashed on his property, blasted into the air by some of the three million pounds of explosives then used every working day in Appalachia. Even though it was blatantly illegal, his family cemetery was desecrated, with 139 graves of his ancestors pushed over the new precipice created by mountaintop removal.

With good humor and moving illustrations, Larry told what mountaintop removal was doing to his land. We listened intently. He might have had only a fifth-grade education, but this man was truly educated—he knew what he was talking about, and his stories made us laugh. "I just finished speaking at Harvard and Yale," he reported. "Then I was at Union Theological Seminary in New York, and in the front row was this big seminary student. I jumped onto his lap, pointed my finger at his head as though my finger were a gun, and said, 'How would you like it if somebody did this to you?'" After he got over being shocked, the big man exploded with laughter. Then Larry said, "Why do you have to step on people's toes before you can get their attention? If I actually shot you, that would be murder, but that's what they're doing in Appalachia—killing people slowly.

"When I started to speak out, they tried to intimidate me, but I never knew you would sacrifice your own beliefs because of intimidation. When threats didn't work, they tried to kill me, like that night at Kayford Mountain when somebody fired repeatedly into my cabin and I saved myself by lying in my iron bathtub! You have to stay cool and calm. Finally, nobody beats you except you!

"My people pay a high price," Larry continued. "For what? Profit! We said to the Appalachian Regional Commission, which is an adviser to the president, 'If it's illegal, why are they doing it? It's okay to break the law if there's profit?' We hear about tragedies happening around the world, but we are not looking at our own tragedy. What's the benefit to you if you destroy your backyard? I can almost hear the land breathing, talking to me. Neither of us destroyed the other because of the respect we have for each other. There are other ways. We're putting people in harm's way because of profit. *The price is too high.*"

As I listened to Larry, I realized I was in the presence of someone who crossed boundaries of race and class to bring people together. By the time he finished his message, I knew that coal mining was destroying beautiful mountains and the people who lived there, and that I had to do something to help. It occurred to me that Larry's words came directly from our Maker and Redeemer. He said, "Change how you live. Stop selling out. Become what you were made to be, a life-giver. I didn't come here to entertain you." He ended his message by saying, "Decide right now. Give what you can. Come down and help us!"

Following his presentation, during the time for conversation, Larry came up to me and said, "Owen, I want you to do my biography."

Surprised, I paused a moment as thoughts raced through my mind: "I'm in my late seventies. I've done a lot of writing, and I probably could do Larry's biography, but it would take a lot of research to do it right. I'm not up to it. I feel honored that Larry trusts me so much. I'll see what I can do."

"Larry," I replied, "I can't write your biography, but I'll see that it gets done!" Months passed, but in the back of my mind remained the promise I made to Larry. Then Allen Johnson, who, after being challenged by Larry, started Christians for the Mountains, wrote,

> Larry Gibson, "Keeper of the Mountains," died Sunday Sept. 9 [2012] at his home on Kayford Mountain, W.V. He was 66. His wife and three adult children survive. Gibson had a fifth-grade education, a career as a custodian at an Ohio automobile factory, and retired to the obscure and abandoned place of his birth. Larry stood 5' 2" . . . .
>
> Gibson made it his passion to "keep" the mountains. His trademark attire was his blaze yellow sweatshirt and cap, "Keeper of the Mountains," at countless protests, rallies, lectures, even coat-and-tie affairs. His pickup truck was festooned with bumper stickers. His outspoken views evoked numerous assaults and acts of vandalism. Undaunted, Larry Gibson always chose the path of integrity over a life of security and ease. His answering machine's message, "*We are the keepers of the mountains. Love them or leave them; just don't destroy them. If you dare to be a keeper, too, call. . . .*"[2]

Allen also wanted Larry's biography written, so we started working together. After several years of gathering materials and approaching qualified biographers who knew Larry but were unable to take on the demanding task, Allen spent two days with my wife, Irene, and me at our home in Kendal Crosslands Communities, working on a prospectus for the book. We agreed we needed a writer who knew Larry well, resonated with him, brought out the flavor of his personality, and wrote in a popular style. A well-written book flowing with a conversational, story-telling style would sell. Since Larry Gibson's life bridged the divisions separating Americans, his story had to get out to a wide audience and therefore needed a publisher whose editor would polish the book and who had the connections and commitment to market it effectively. Allen called Marybeth Lorbiecki, biographer, writer, and member of the Religious Coalition for Creation Care, and she agreed to write Larry's biography.

Ever since Larry asked me to write his biography, I had intended to go to southern West Virginia and see Kayford Mountain and the devastated land. At age eighty-six, I needed somebody to drive with me, and on Wednesday, June 16, 2021, my son Martin and I traveled through West Virginia's beautiful mountains on our way to the state capital, Charleston, where Allen had arranged for us to stay at the Saint John XXIII Pastoral Center, a Catholic retreat. Early on Thursday, I got in Allen's car to drive to Kayford Mountain. Beside the road up the hollow to Larry's place was a small creek. It was off-color and looked unhealthy, and Japanese knotweed covered its banks to where the kudzu cascaded up the trees on the forest edge. The farther up we went, the worse the road. When the blacktop ended, Allen drove slowly to avoid potholes and rocks. Next to the road's edge was a slope so steep I was amazed that trees could grow on it, but there they were. Finally, we reached the top of Kayford Mountain. "There's Larry's cabin," Allen pointed out, "and there are the vacation places of his family."

The striking beauty of Coal River Mountain loomed across from us as we walked a path to the end of Larry's land. A bulldozed wall of rubble blocked the trail. "Can you climb up this?" Allen asked.

"Yes, I can if I'm careful," I replied as we edged ourselves up to the top. We stood up, and as I looked straight down at a ninety-degree slope, I realized that where we were standing was part of a mountain ridge that had been entirely blasted away. Far below was the flat, almost barren moonscape of the "reclaimed" land.

At my feet were deep tracks—thrill seekers must have ridden four-wheelers right down that precipice hundreds of feet to the plain below! Four-wheeler tracks also wove across the flattened land, clearly doing no good to the struggling bits of vegetation. The place looked like Montana, not West Virginia, and suddenly in my mind's eye I saw wood bison and elk grazing, their droppings fertilizing now barren earth (these ungulates once thrived throughout Appalachia before settlers exterminated the herds). I could see four-wheelers with eco-tourists taking pictures of wood bison, elk, and the wolves that accompanied the herds—maybe restoration of this desecrated land could open new jobs, as it had in Kentucky.[3]

We walked back to Larry's grave on the hill just above his cabin. The gravestone read: *My mother gave me birth. The land gave me life.* Allen and I prayed, thanking the Lord for Larry and all he gave to bring life back to this land and its people.

At lunchtime, we sat at a picnic table under the tin roof that had been used many times in Larry's family celebrations. Vandals had stripped out the electrical wire. A few planks were pulled out of the tables, but it wouldn't take much work to put things back together. Across from us was the covered bandstand where singers and speakers once stirred the people.

Larry had saved Kayford Mountain from destruction, but it seemed lonely. Allen and I walked up the eroded road to the three crosses to which Allen had helped Larry clear the view the week before Larry died. Helping hands were needed again, not only to keep the view of the crosses clear but also to close the eroding four-wheeler trail somebody had slashed near the existing road and plant trees on it. There were no signs of the organization that Larry had started to carry on his work. I felt that somebody needed to live here, growing their food, catching water from the sky, building new life together on this solid West Virginia foundation, and reaching out to the world with Larry's message that the land gives life.

On Friday morning, Allen and I met Maria Gunnoe and Chuck Nelson, who would take us through Twilight Mine, the largest mountaintop removal site on the East Coast. We climbed into Maria's pickup truck, and soon we arrived at where we were to register to enter the mine. Maria had called ahead. The guard handed us forms to fill in and sign. After he checked the paperwork, he said, "Now you have to agree not to take pictures until you get to Jarrell Cemetery, but there you can go to the edges and use your cameras." Then he handed us a mobile phone and speaker so we could keep in touch with the truck that was to escort us through the mine. A dusty pickup appeared, and we followed it up the unpaved, dusty road.

After pulling over to let a coal truck pass, we soon reached an immense plateau. A seam of exposed coal was being mined, but the operation was small. The huge draglines were gone. Massey Energy Company, once the sixth-largest producer of coal in the United States, employing almost six thousand miners while operating thirty-five underground mines and twelve surface mines, was gone too. Alpha Natural Resources bought out Massey after settling Massey's potential criminal liabilities for flagrant safety violations at a cost of $209 million.[4]

The pickup led us across a dusty land. "When dynamite explodes, silicone dust fills the air. When you breathe it, you get silicosis," Maria explained.

Though the windows were closed and the air-conditioning was on, I sensed I was inhaling dust. "Imagine what it was like to work here," I reflected, "or live near this mine when it was going full force."

"After the coal was dug out, it had to be washed with water and toxic chemicals," Maria said. "In one valley, bulldozers shoved rocks, rubble, and logs together to make a dam higher than the Hoover Dam. Behind that dam, they pumped water filled with whatever washed off the coal—mercury, sludge, cleaning chemicals. I know about at least twenty such ponds, and there are probably more waiting for a big storm to lock in place, dump inches of rain, break the dam, and flood everyone and everything below it. The Mother Jones Community Foundation submitted a funding proposal seeking mine remediation funds, first, to set up an early warning system so that when a dam breaks, people can escape the flood; second, to get the huge lakes dewatered safely; and third, to mine rare earth minerals in the sludge deposits without causing more damage."

We came to a winding one-lane road to Jarrell Cemetery's wooded pinnacle. "As soon as the mine closes, the road goes to the county," Maria noted. "We sued Massey because they ignored the boundary and mined to the edge of where people are buried. The hundred-thousand-dollar settlement will help pay a little of the cost of maintaining the road."

We parked where the road ended, got out, and walked to the neatly mowed grass of the cemetery. A grave that stood out to me was that of a World War II veteran. "He died in Italy," Chuck said. "They brought him up here with a horse-drawn wagon and had a full ceremony laying him to rest."

"We won't go to look over the edge," Maria said. "I don't have my snake boots on. This cemetery was the only place left where rattlesnakes could flee, and there are quite a few in the little bit of forest around us."

After taking pictures and holding hands in prayer, Maria called the woman in the pickup, and she led us down the hill back to the guardhouse.

"How much would the guard and pickup driver earn?" I asked.

"Remember, Massey Coal broke the United Mine Workers' Union," Maria responded. "The pickup driver earns ten or eleven dollars per hour; the guard, a little more." We saw no coal trucks on the way out—mining was indeed winding down.

Maria and Chuck took us to one of the few remaining coffee shops. "Mining coal underground was dangerous and hard," Chuck shared. "It was a boom-and-bust industry, and yet these communities that grew up in the hollows were good places to live. The mountains were beautiful. We walked through the woods. One fellow knew every squirrel tree on the mountain. Now the trees and the mountain I knew are gone. When they started mountaintop mining, they bought people out of those areas and tore their houses down. When they scraped clean areas along creeks, they hydroseeded Japanese knotweed, which spread downstream, killing off the native plants. Many who stayed got cancer, emphysema, and other sicknesses from poisons in the water and air."

"The mountaintop removal area we saw today was vast," I said. "Before I came here, I had no idea how big it was."

"The last step in planning a mountaintop removal coal mine is to review site plans by the West Virginia DEP," Maria responded. "They adjust the boundaries to minimize visibility from the main roads."

Saturday night, Martin, Allen, and I watched the 2016 film *Blood on the Mountains*, about southern West Virginia's history from the viewpoint of the people who lived here, worked the mines, and built lasting communities. Energy in coal stored for countless millennia was mined to power expanding industries. As coal companies got bigger, the successful ones excelled in making as much profit as they could from land and labor. When times were good, men came to work in the booming mines. Then came the "bust" depressions when jobs dried up. Ruthless owners exploited miners in every conceivable way, including paying in scrip that could only be spent at company stores. When a man was too injured to work again or was killed in an accident, the overseer threw the family out of the company house in which they lived so a new hand could move in and keep the mine going. Likewise, when mines played out, big companies sold what was left to little operators who soon went bankrupt. As the owners foresaw, the mining company escaped liability for cleaning up despoiled and polluted land and paying pension and health care costs for the silicosis, black lung disease, and cancers of the miners who had labored for them.

Think of the self-sacrifice of those who have tried to organize a union, stop mountaintop removal, and revitalize Appalachia's economies. Light seemed to glimmer at the end of the mine tunnel, and then it all got even darker. When there seems to be no hope, what can we do?

The Fear of the Lord Is the Beginning of Wisdom

Nature is shaped by predator and prey relationships, in which fear and terror are lifesaving. A rabbit that ignores the approach of a hawk, or when it is seen, freezes in despair, invites death. Fear and terror also touch human relationships. Suppose somebody holds your paycheck in his hand and says, "If you want to keep your job, you'd better see those kooks who want to stop mountaintop removal shut up!" Suppose you run for public office and "the man" says, "If I give you a big campaign contribution, you can help support the coal industry!" We fear a tyrant's weapons of control—loss, exile, torture, death. Sometimes fear moves us to seek liberty and justice for all, but most of the time it leads us to conform to the "big man" who dictates, "Do this or else!"

Where there is no vision, the people unravel (an interpretation of Proverbs 29:18). Taken advantage of when we work hard to make a living and support our families, whom can we trust? Seeing once familiar mountains and forests turned to rubble, we wonder, "Who's on our side?" We see the "big man" who runs the company automate and drastically reduce the number of people who work for him, buy off legislators who could stop mountaintop removal, and divide and conquer those who seek to unite and organize exploited people. Going to rallies, we hear a rich, powerful speaker tell us to back him and hate the liberals and foreigners, and we ask, "Who speaks for me?"

Biblical prophets tell us the people are unraveling, and creation is collapsing because human beings have decided to ignore the divinely given bonds that hold people and nature together. The apostle Paul tells us we have sinned and fallen short of God's glory, failing to live as truly human beings. When we sin against the Lord, breaking the Lord's family values, the Ten Commandments, and seem to get away with it, we wall ourselves off from love and light.

All too soon comes the day when we die. Our body is gone—we can no longer touch, grab hold, or do anything. Surrounded by the cold, hard darkness that we have used to hide what we were doing and get what we wanted—no matter who got hurt, we find ourselves intensely aware of all we have said and done. We see the land mourning, see the miners dying from black lung disease we could have prevented, see children who would have grown up to be somebody had we not automated away their jobs, see the women who could have loved us had we not grabbed, groped, and sexually assaulted them. After a lifetime of decisions to live in darkness, lost souls wonder, "Is there any hope for me?"

Facing a bleak future, more than superficial encouragement is necessary. When I visit someone near death after all treatment has failed, I feel helpless. Then I remember Emmanuel, God with us, and that strengthens me to be with that person, listen, and pray with him or her. Light dawns even when we walk through the valley of the shadow of death, because the Light of life is with us. The Lord, who is just and loving, hears the agonized cries of dead, lost souls. We must leave what happens to folks who destroyed the mountains and exploited the people in the hands of the Almighty and Merciful One.

Right now the Holy Spirit calls us to decide to let go and let God, trusting the Lord to care for us and guide us. Suppose we open ourselves to the surrounding presence of the Holy One who called us into being. Jesus taught us not to fear those who can kill the body but instead to fear the One who can destroy both soul and body (Matthew 10:28). When primal creative light shines on us and we feel its stern electrical energies, who would not be terrified? Instead of fearing and wanting to be like people who are rich, famous, and powerful; instead of believing "he's somebody and I'm nobody," we must believe Christ when he says, *You are somebody special. I know when one little sparrow falls to the ground. I made you, I know you, I love you, and I want you to be who I created you to be. Live and love right now!*

Prophets who have seen the Lord tell us the Lord loves those who love kindness, do justice, and walk humbly with their God. Jesus Christ longs for us to live this way and be who we were created to be—truly human beings. When we fear the Lord, we begin to become wise. We see we don't need to be "the man," be with "the man," or try to live like that celebrity anymore. Now we are humble enough to ask, seek, and knock.

When we fear the Lord, who creates and redeems, the Holy Spirit immerses us in living water. We die to the old self and become who we were made to be. Turning from the way of death to the way of life is a hard choice. One who made that choice was Chuck Nelson. When we were with him, traveling across the Twilight Mine, he shared that he saw the communities in which he grew up being disintegrated by the new way of mining. "I'm not against coal miners," he told us. "I was a miner and worked hard to support my family. When I saw communities destroyed by the mining company, I decided I had to do what I could to stop mountaintop removal."

Like a mother giving a drink to a thirsty child, the Spirit of the Lord pours out amazing gifts on all who will receive: wisdom, knowledge, understanding, fear of the Lord, power, guidance, and discernment. Some who step out into the light are religious, like Isaiah, a priest who became a prophet when he saw the Lord in the

Jerusalem temple. Others are people like Larry Gibson, who for many years lived like "the man," and then saw that while his mother gave him birth, it was Kayford Mountain that gave him life. Larry asked people like Ken Hechler, an honest elder of West Virginia politics, to teach him what he had to do to save the land. He applied what he learned, sometimes succeeding, sometimes failing, learning more and more as he spoke truth to those in power, as he did that day I experienced at Cabrini College.

Come and Help Us

When mining companies release their bloody grip on Boone County, the number one priority is gaining power to know best how to restore the land, water, and people. After mining ends, whoever owns the land has immense liabilities—that's why Big Coal sells out to little operators and they go bankrupt. Maybe for a few years nobody will want these wasted lands. Who wants to own a rubble dam impounding an immense, toxic lake, which is waiting for an eight-inch rainstorm to break it and flood down on people? *Blood on the Mountains* shows amazing resistance by West Virginians and others from Appalachia over many generations to exploitation. How do committed local leaders build up caring, regenerative communities and help them to gain control of what's happening and to maintain control seven generations down?

We can learn a lot from Larry Gibson as we move forward.

- Larry came back home to Kayford Mountain and brought all he had learned to bear on a seemingly impossible task—saving the land that gave him birth.
- Larry brought his extended family together with celebrations at Kayford Mountain—people shared and ate good food, laughed and joked, listened to music, heard stimulating, challenging speakers, and talked about what was happening.

- Larry talked directly with each member of his family—at celebrations, in phone calls and visits, asking them to put their part of the land they inherited at Kayford Mountain into a special foundation he started to save the mountain.
- Larry refused to play the "tree of good and evil knowledge" game, in which he would see himself and his people "right" and others "wrong"—with him, it was not "my way or the highway."
- Larry sought out people who could help, no matter who they were—rich or poor, colored or white, Republican or Democrat—and listened to and learned from them.
- Larry spoke out against mountaintop removal mining and continued to do so when he was threatened, when an attempt was made on his life, and when he was jailed.
- Larry organized, joined, and led demonstrations.
- Larry testified to legislators and the governor in Charleston, West Virginia, and to senators and representatives in Washington, DC.
- Larry kept and deepened his faith in Christ, as in the last week of his life, when he cleared away brush obscuring the three crosses he had placed on the hill.
- Larry called people from all over the country and asked them to do what he himself had done—"Come over and help us."

Light shines from Boone County, West Virginia. The mountains and people of this county show what happens when money-making development at any cost is pursued to its end. If the industrial, urban expansion of "civilization" continues at its disastrous pace, a few years from now the whole planet will look like the Twilight Mine and its surrounding area. These dark realities might make the future appear hopeless except for those brave women and men in West Virginia who spoke truth and lived in the light—long before coal mining started, through the mining years, and down to the present:

- For millennia Cherokees and other tribes shared and maintained a bountiful "common pot" of nature and have many lessons to teach about forming regenerative communities.[5]
- Though the disastrous Trail of Tears took many Cherokees to Oklahoma, bands of Cherokees and other tribes avoided the attempted genocide, kept their language and ancestral traditions alive, and continue to live in their mountains and valleys, today possessing experientially derived wisdom about how to survive and live in balance with nature and people.
- Waves of Anglo-Americans coming through Appalachia liked what they found and homesteaded, with peaceful interactions and intermarriage as well as fighting shaping relations between Cherokees and new settlers, forming a distinctive subculture of North America whose language, music, art, and crafts continue to enrich the nation.
- Extended families with aunts, uncles, and cousins keep in touch with each other and hallow the gravesites of relatives who birthed and made life today possible—communities are still very much alive.
- Boone County shares with Appalachia resistance to tyranny, whether from massive corporations or government bodies managed far away who take all they can and give little back.
- Miners sweated in dark, underground tunnels, survived rock falls and explosions, and made a living. Their wives reared the children with them, and they worked together to organize unions and build supportive families and communities.
- Independent-minded churches preach, sing, and teach, giving hope and strength, and their buildings provide a place for community meetings.

There are many ways we can respond to Larry's call to come and help:

- Respect and listen to West Virginia leaders such as Larry, Maria, Chuck, and Allen. We have much to learn from those in a land that has been conquered and the people ruthlessly exploited yet moving forward to restore human and natural life.
- Unite by recognizing we're all in this together. As missionaries learned, we indeed come down, get to know people, and let the Spirit guide us as to what support is necessary.
- Share what we have learned, as well as our abilities and resources. When we give as we have been blessed, energy is released that lifts and builds up.

There are, of course, kinds of help people can do without, as Larry experienced when his parents moved to Cleveland and bought him new boots, overalls, and a shirt to wear for his first day at the school near their home. Larry was proud of his new clothes as he entered the fifth-grade classroom. The teacher, however, saw that this boy was a "hillbilly" who didn't even know how to dress right to come to class, and asked the class to have their parents donate old clothes for Larry. Humiliated but proud, Larry never went back to school.

A regenerate, caring community comes into being when we realize all living beings are on a journey through life together. Everyone is unique and uniquely important. To live and to live well, creatures of God must do these things:

- Eat nourishing food.
- Drink, bathe, and wash in clean water.
- Breathe pure, oxygenated air.
- See and hear the sights of beauty around and in us.
- Have a safe place to live.
- Belong to a community of family and friends.
- Decide to walk and learn to move forward on the way of life.

Underground mining has polluted and poisoned land and people. Extending strip mining to remove whole mountains and dump the rubble into valleys is devastating Appalachia. Where could you find a bigger environmental challenge than southern West Virginia? And where else for so long have people spoken out, organized unions, and fought for safe mining, fair pay, clean water and air, homegrown food, and good schools? Restoration of the land and of the human communities that endured is the key that unlocks the door to better days ahead.

To that end, the Boone County Mother Jones Community Foundation has submitted a proposal to the federal government for mine reclamation funds to remediate dangerous toxic waste dams by setting up an early warning system, safely dewatering the lake, and getting rid of the toxic waste on the bottom. They have also been in touch with Steve Apfelbaum, head of Resource Environmental Solutions, LLC (RES), the nation's largest ecological restoration company focused on restoring a resilient earth for a modern world, seeking help in restoring nature in Boone County. They have also connected with Trout Unlimited, seeking cleanup and revitalization of the county's streams and rivers, and created a community garden program, which in its initial years has many growing fresh food.

A new day is dawning. We are being called by prophets like Mari Lynn Evans, Larry Gibson, Maria Gunnoe, Chuck Nelson, and a host of others to help Appalachian people save their land. Are changes for the better possible? Can people without power and money do anything? Look what happened when one person in Boone County started "Pennies for Schools." It took years, but now children go to a new school safer from floods, toxic air, and water pollution. West Virginia leaders who have stood up and spoken out to rescue the perishing and restore the earth will see the Lord open new opportunities and will move forward as they are led.

Conclusion

If the earth's wildlife, forests, rivers, and oceans continue to sicken and die, we will all go down with a fossil-fuel-fired planetary ship. But we can discover that God's love lights the way into better days ahead. Maybe someone who has made money using cheap electricity from coal-fired plants wants to pay back some of the debt owed to people and land in a "natural sacrifice zone." Maybe many little somebodies will contribute to a nonprofit foundation to protect, preserve, and restore southern West Virginia and build up local businesses with diverse sources of income in a digital era. Maybe you are being called, as I have been, to give what you can to support pioneers who are leading us to restore mined-out wastelands.

We know how Larry Gibson would end this message: "I didn't come here to entertain you. Come join us in saving our people and land, and we will move forward together."

Notes

1. On March 11, 2010, I took field notes as Larry Gibson gave his message. I have drawn on those notes for the following paragraphs.

2. Allen Johnson, "Larry Gibson, Keeper of the Mountains," *Sojourners*, October 12, 2012, https://sojo.net/articles/larry-gibson-keeper-mountains.

3. In strip-mined areas of Kentucky, elk have been reestablished by landowners working with conservationists and the Kentucky Department of Fish & Wildlife, bringing in income from eco-tourism and hunting. After a concerted reintroduction effort two decades ago, the state of Kentucky is now home to the largest population of elk east of the Mississippi. The animals' home is reclaimed strip and mountaintop removal coal mines. "Elk Return to Kentucky, Bringing Economic Life," *New York Times*, June 20, 2020.

4. Massey Energy owned and operated Upper Big Branch Mine where twenty-nine miners were killed in April 2010. The Mine Safety and Health Administration found that the company's culture of favoring production over safety contributed to flagrant safety violations that caused the coal dust explosion. On December 6, 2011, the Mine Safety and Health Administration announced a $10,825,368 levy against Massey, the largest monetary penalty imposed by the agency in history. The resulting $10.8 million in total was from 369 citations and orders. Following Alpha Natural Resources' acquisition, Alpha additionally settled Massey's potential criminal liabilities for $209 million. See Amy Louviere,

MSHA Press Release, Mine Safety and Health Administration of the US Department of Labor, accessed July 17, 2025, https://web.archive.org/web/20120111174845/http://www.msha.gov/MEDIA/PRESS/2011/NR111206.asp.

5. Daniel H. Justice, *Our Fire Survives the Storm: A Cherokee Literary History* (University of Minnesota Press, 2006); Lisa Brooks, *The Common Pot: The Recovery of Native Space in the Northeast* (University of Minnesota Press, 2008).

CHAPTER 2

Enlighten Our Minds

In the stained glass window of a Chicago chapel shines the yellow and green of a sunflower. "Why the sunflower?" I asked a nun.

"For the early Christians, the sunflower was a symbol of faith," she replied. "Each morning it faces the sun, absorbing the warm light, which gives it energy. Throughout the day, the plant follows the sun, and the next morning it again faces east, waiting for the first beams of sunlight."

Powerful energy comes when we question, explore, and learn. When we decide to live in the light, the Holy Spirit with compassionate wisdom floods our minds and hearts, and what we say and do bears witness to the everlasting Light.

Learn—Let the Sunshine In

When we question and explore, we learn and grow. One hot and humid afternoon, even an avid fisherman like me had to sit down on a log to rest. In the riffle above me, a little boy played in the water, throwing stones, exploring, and touching tiny creatures scraped from the stream's bottom and placed in his little bucket with the gentle assistance of his mother. After a while, seeing rising trout, I waded into the pool a little above them. A few minutes later, the boy and his mother appeared on the trail near me.

"He wanted to see what you are doing," she said in a calm, melodious voice.

"Well, I'm fishing for trout with a fly that looks like an ant—here it is." I showed them the fly, we talked for a moment, and then the mother took her son back into the stream before leaving for home.

Reflecting on that day took me back to being a curious child. I wanted to learn, understand, and know, while constantly asking questions. Do you remember doing that too? "What is that? What's its name? Why do you do that?" Patient family members answered as best they could and encouraged me to keep wondering and questioning because I would learn this way. I remember the delight when an answer came and I understood.

The little boy in the stream was guided by a wise mother as he explored his growing power by using his head, hands, lips, ears, nose, and fingertips. By so doing, he entered the company of every child back to the beginning of time. Being in the stream on that humid afternoon introduced him to living water, an experience he would need in the years ahead.

Remember the pure joy that came when you learned something difficult? Something in me makes mathematics forbidding, but everyone preparing for college was required to take the plane geometry class taught by Miss Laura Wagner, who taught us to think. Soon my classmates and I were caught up in each problem she presented, seeking to get an answer and to understand the process. Sometimes I was ready to give up in despair, but the hope that I might "get it" kept me studying and struggling. Then suddenly, unexpectedly, I would perceive the answer and be able to explain how I arrived at it. What a delight! One day I said to myself, "Oh my, I'm thinking! So that's why we work so hard to learn something." Laura Wagner showed us that we had undreamed-of capacities to learn and grow.

When I think about being wise, I remember my grandmother, Mary Boltz Bieck. Her father came to Rome, Wisconsin, from Leimersheim, Germany. She grew up in a farming community, and though she had only a grade school education, her understanding went deep. Friends and family would come to her with a worrying concern, saying, "Mary, this is taking me down. What should I do?" Grandma would listen, ask for more information, and let more light shine in until the issues were clear to her. Then she would say, "Let me pray about this and sleep on it. Often something will come to me, and then we'll talk."

Sure enough, a new day's light brought helpful insight, which she shared with the one seeking her help. They would talk, thinking things through until a way forward became clear for the seeker. Then he or she would pray, decide what to do, carry the action through, and learn from what happened. In other words, when light shone through this wise woman, the one seeking help became a little wiser too.

The Hebrew and Christian Scriptures teach that the fear of the Lord is the beginning of wisdom. Undergirding this teaching is the Creator's intent to restore the creation covenant described in Genesis 1, and you and me! Bill W., founder of Alcoholics Anonymous, after uncontrollable drinking, found himself sick, in a hospital bed, shaking with delirium tremens—he was going to die! He hit bottom. In despair he cried for help. Suddenly warm, personal light flooded the room, and he knew he would not drink again. He also knew he would give his life to help others find sobriety. Suddenly awe, fear, and love ignited his decision to live and share what he was given with others.

A voice is speaking to you and to me, saying, *You are caught, trapped—turn to me and live!*

"Who are you, Lord?"

I am the One who will free you to live fully and wisely—right now and forever.

"How do I do that, Lord?"

Let go of what you are holding on to and trust me to take care of you—I will provide all you need.

"I can't do that, Lord. Where I work the boss is in charge, and he aims to make as much money as fast as he can for the company and himself. If I want to make a living, I must do what he says.

I'm scared—what will happen to me and my family if I let go?"

What you're holding on to is falling apart right before your eyes. Nothing and no one I've created lasts long. With me is the fountain of life. Put your fears on me. I made you in my own image, and you are precious to me. When you die, I will take you back to myself.[1]

"But I've had no experience of you. I don't read the Bible and almost never pray."

Go to your roots in nature and the faith of your ancestors. Enter a natural place near you, look at what's happening, and listen to the sounds—what you people call wilderness is my original and enduring temple. And go to the rock from which you were hewn—why would I repeat what I said and did with Abraham and Sarah, Miriam and Moses, Jesus and the disciples? Learn to worship, pray, eat, and study together with others. You'll need all the help you can get when you restore your connection to your branch of God's people. As light shines on and in you, never forget there is one tree of life—I want people of all faiths to come together to rescue the perishing and restore the earth. When you're ready, I'll show you the way forward.

Alexander Humboldt and Wisdom

Alexander Humboldt studied, explored, and became an enlightened person. Until I read his biography, I never knew that he was a person who shaped the ecology-justice vision that has informed me. After years of yearning to see the New World, Humboldt left Spain in 1799, bound for South America:

> Like previous explorers, he would collect plants, seeds, rocks and animals. He would measure the height of mountains, determine longitude and latitude, and take temperatures of water and air. But the real purpose of the voyage, he said, was to discover how "all forces of nature are inter-

> acted and interwoven"—how organic and inorganic nature interacted. Man needs to strive for "the good and the great" Humboldt wrote in his last letter from Spain, "the rest depends on destiny."[2]

Humboldt and his companion, Aimé Bonpland, departed from Caracas, Venezuela, starting their travels in the Aragua valleys, one of the wealthiest agricultural regions in the Spanish colonies. Humboldt learned that Lake Valencia's water level was dropping precipitously, and people wondered why that was happening. He measured and observed what happened when forests were cut. As the land wore out and water dried up, planters moved west, leaving a trail of ruined lands behind them. Slaves cleared away forests and worked the land. Humboldt was appalled by the slave market he visited—a child of the Enlightenment, he was convinced that all people were equal. Throughout his long life, he spoke out for the emancipation of slaves.

At Lake Valencia Humboldt developed his understanding that human beings were changing the climate. From Aristotle to Descartes and Bacon, philosophers believed nature existed to be subdued and used by human beings, and that "orderly fields, cleared forests, and neat villages turned a savage wilderness into pleasing and productive landscapes."[3] Humboldt, to the contrary, realized that the planters were *using up* land and people. He saw slaves logging the forests and tilling the fields, but it was the Spanish colonists who got rich. In his letters back to the salons and drawing rooms of Europe, he told how colonial plantations took land from the native tribes, oppressed the African slaves, and destroyed the ecosystems from which they were created. Genocide, slavery, and ecocide were caused by the expansion of European nations through conquests of land and people.

After months of travel and strenuous explorations, Humboldt left Quito with his three companions to ride through thick tropical vegetation toward Chimborazo, a "monstrous colossus" of a snow-capped volcano.[4] Day after day, he scanned the mountain through his telescope, awed by its snowy peak against a vibrant blue sky. As he got closer and ascended open grassy plains, he could see a barren, boulder-covered landscape around Chimborazo.

An expert mountain climber, Humboldt had explored every peak anywhere close to his travel route, yet the prospect of ascending Chimborazo was daunting. On June 22, 1802, Humboldt and his companions, assisted by a group of porters from a village near the mountain, rode on mules across grass-covered slopes until they reached 13,500 feet. They continued on foot as the temperature grew colder. It had snowed on Chimborazo the night before, and the summit was fog-covered. At 15,600 feet, the porters refused to go any farther, but for Humboldt, what appeared unreachable exerted a mysterious pull. The four companions divided the instruments among them and climbed upward, even crawling along a two-inch-wide ridge with chasms yawning on both sides! Hands and feet were numb from the cold. Altitude sickness made their eyes bloodshot and their gums bleed. Even worse, they were nauseous and dizzy. Humboldt later acknowledged their dangerous situation.

Yet, again and again, he would get out the chilled instruments with half-frozen hands to record air and ground temperature, collect air samples, and push down rocks to see how far they went before they stopped. They left the "knife edge" only to be climbing across rocks so sharp they cut through their boots. With bleeding, numb feet, they continued up to 19,413 feet. Only 1,000 feet below the summit, they were blocked by an immense crevasse and an impassable snow field. They could go no farther.

Hard, risky climbing and rigorous scientific study opened the door to new learning; then insight came as a gift. Higher than any European had ever been before, the fog cleared. After gazing in awe at the shining peak, Humboldt looked down from Chimborazo to the mountain ranges in the distance. Suddenly all he had learned about rocks, plants, forests, and Alpine mountains fell into place: "Nature, Humboldt realized, was a web of life and a global force. He was, a colleague later said, the first to understand that everything was interwoven as with 'a thousand threads.' This new idea of nature was to change the ways people understood the world."[5]

Plants at the same altitude on different continents resembled each other. He saw below him climate zones very similar to those that ranged from the tropics to the frigid poles. Like the monks who opened God's book of nature by going into the wilderness and discovering all that was there, Humboldt risked his life, pulled forward by a sense of mysteries to be discovered.

> The plant groups ranged from the tropical species down in the valleys to the lichens that he had encountered near the snow line. Towards the end of his life, Humboldt often talked about understanding nature from a "higher point of view" from which those connections could be seen. The moment when he had realized this was here, on Chimborazo. With "a single glance," he saw the whole of nature laid out before him.[6]

In his later years, Humboldt not only laid the foundations for the scientific study of mountains, glaciers, oceans, and tropical and temperate ecosystems but also connected human *feelings and imagination* with empirical observation and measurement, creating a blueprint for nature writers following in his footsteps. His letters and books told stories of his travels and of the beauty and wonder of the teeming life in the wild places he visited. He brought what he felt as well as what he saw—for instance, describing constantly changing rainbows in a waterfall, as well as measuring gradient and volume as best he could with the instruments he laboriously carried with him. Readers loved his writings, which lifted them for a while out of a warring world into exciting adventures in wild nature.[7]

Alexander Humboldt has much to teach us about enlightening our minds. We who are religious also have a cosmic vision (read Psalm 147). Humboldt did not practice religion, and yet his visionary research and writings have blessed us in myriad ways. Those who follow in the train of Moses and the prophets, Jesus and the apostolic churches, and Muhammad and the worldwide Muslim movement need to cease ignoring painful ecology-justice realities and open our minds to what is happening to planet Earth's climate and all life upon it, and seek to contribute to a more just and ecologically whole world.

Humboldt shows us that truth emerges when we use every means available to us to learn, spending our money and taking risks, drawn by the mysterious pull to understand that which seems to be unreachable. We also learn from his experience what mystics of all traditions teach, namely, that wisdom is a gift from the mysteries that brought into being all that is and shaped life on earth. All he learned from his travel, disciplined research, and persistent dialogue with each person he met came together when he looked down—not up—and saw in an instant that the earth had climate zones! Even more, in that moment of perception, he saw that all life was interwoven.

Humboldt saw that European plantations were based on genocide—taking land from native peoples by any means necessary; slavery—abusing whip-driven laborers to cut down the forests and work the land; and ecocide—replacing ecosystems with monoculture agriculture. Over the 220 years since Humboldt, changes have been made. Human slavery was ended, but the plantation system continued with machines powered by fossil fuel doing much of the labor. Now a great deal of the carbon emissions producing climate change come from agribusiness plantations, processing systems, packaging, and transportation. Continued destruction of ecosystems has created an immense wave of extinction, sweeping large and small creatures into oblivion.

Jesus said that wisdom is justified by all her children (Matthew 11:19). Facing a future in which the climate and ecological systems are disintegrating, and hosts of refugees are seeking a safe place to live, we need all the help we can get. Alexander Humboldt was indeed a child of wisdom. The great professor still has much to teach us.

Receive the Sevenfold Gifts of Wisdom

Humboldt's necessary changes—end slavery, genocide, and eco-cide—challenge us to draw on the work of Bible scholars, theologians, and ethicists who have addressed these concerns. As I ascended the Museum of the Acropolis walkway in Greece for the first session of Archbishop Bartholomew's 2018 Greening Attica conference, I met Margaret Barker, and we started to talk. When we reached the top, Margaret said, "Owen, I want to convert you to Temple Mysticism!" Now, I had no idea what Temple Mysticism was, but I did learn that Margaret brought Bible scholarship to bear on caring for the environment.

Intrigued by conversion to something of which I had never heard, I read Margaret's books *Temple Mysticism* and *Creation* when I returned home. Both books were deeply informed not only by Hebrew and Christian Scriptures but also by the Dead Sea Scrolls and intertestamental literature. She states that two traditions have shaped our understanding of the Scriptures, one creation-based, the other history-based.[8] The creation-based Temple Mysticism tradition centers on the eternal covenant with creation established on day one when God made heaven and earth, whereas the history-based tradition centers on the exodus from Egypt and God's giving the Law to Moses on Mount Sinai. Though the unraveling of the natural order requires spiritual as well as scientific attention, over the past two hundred years, the men who studied and taught the Bible saw God speaking and acting in history and tended to neglect and obscure creation-based spirituality within Christian and Hebrew Scriptures.[9]

Drawing on many years of Hebrew and Christian Scripture studies, Margaret Barker helped me see that the creation covenant was established on day one.[10] In Temple Mysticism's biblical tradition, Wisdom was seated on the foundation stone at the center of creation. The Hebrew word for wisdom is feminine, so I use feminine pronouns for her. She was the queen, the woman of the first temple in Jerusalem, who maintained stability and security.[11] Envisioned as the bonds of the covenant and discernment that produced the virtues of justice, righteousness, and harmony, her symbols were the water of life, the bread of the presence, the song of the angels, the anointing oil, and the menorah (probably her stylized tree). Wisdom is the God-given way of knowing the world.

Perhaps we can recover and apply the discoveries of those who went before us. Wisdom comes in material ways. In the ancient tabernacle and temple ceremonies, women prepared the bread for consumption. Water quenched thirst and cleansed. Oils anointed and healed. Branches of trees reminded worshippers of the tree of life from which we cut ourselves off and to which worship restores us. In the ancient temple in Jerusalem, those touched with sacred anointing oil became the children of wisdom, allowing them to see the world differently. Their eyes were opened, initiating the battle between truth and falsehood. Wisdom unites creation and salvation theologies, providing a visionary tradition that takes one into the depths of human life and experience with a complex of teaching lenses:

- The kingdom of God—the holy of holies—is grounded in the everlasting creation covenant, which binds together the entire living world and is expressed in divine directives for ethical living, temple construction, and rituals of worship in this world (Exodus 20–31).

- Wisdom, understood as feminine, is the source of knowledge and understanding: She opens eyes so that people see the vision at the heart of the covenant.
- Wisdom is the mother of the Logos/Messiah.
- Cherubim and angels, unseen powers of the universe, carry messages of God and connect material and spiritual realities.
- The foundation stone of creation on which wisdom is enthroned binds together the forces of nature and enables justice and righteousness, providing a solid, safe rock on which to build our lives (as Jesus teaches in Matthew 7:24-27).
- The river of life flows from God's temple.
- The tree of life bears fruit for the healing of the nations.
- Human beings, created in the divine image of steadfast covenant love, fall into evildoing, injustice, and constant warfare, and are restored through divine atonement, confession of sin, and turning to live in God's kingdom.
- Sound and wise teaching destroys the destroyers of the earth.[12]

Christians in the early church received the sevenfold gifts of the Holy Spirit: wisdom, fear of God, knowledge, counsel, understanding, might, and discernment (Isaiah 11:1-2). When the Spirit came upon the women and men at Pentecost with wind and fire, their tongues were loosed, as happened to the prophet Isaiah, and they spoke in many languages. They not only preached and taught but also built their lives on the foundation stone of wisdom, as Jesus taught us to do in the Sermon on the Mount, which he concluded with this story: "The rain fell, the floods came, and the winds blew and beat on that house, but it did not fall because it had been founded on rock. And everyone who hears these words of mine and does not act on them will be like a foolish man who built his house on sand" (Matthew 7:25-26).

Every moment of life is an opportunity to open yourself intentionally to the sevenfold gifts of the Spirit of Wisdom. Surrounded by the shining presence that formed and sustains us, the Creator's sun shines on everyone. When we pray for light, we turn to the Source of life, who loves everyone, good and evil, righteous and unrighteous, you and me (Psalm 145). The Creator's rain falls on everyone and everything, just and unjust alike, wetting the soil, germinating seeds, and bringing life from the earth (Matthew 5:43-48). Being created in God's image is like being a mirror. When we face the Light, we shine with light. We are created with the divine capacity for rigorous learning that steadfast love calls forth, joining the life-sustaining energies of the creation covenant.[13] When we turn away from God, our light fades into darkness. But when we open our eyes to the light, an amazing thing happens. The holy light of God touches us and lights our fires.

After an afternoon walk following cataract surgery, I sat on a bench overlooking a pond. Though a cold breeze was blowing, the February late afternoon sun shone warmly. Everything looked normal. Outlines of bare-branched trees were reflected on the green-tinted water.

"Well," I said to myself, "let's see what happens when I look through my new lens." The sky was bright blue, and snow on the pond's bank gleamed white with bluish tints. "Amazing," I marveled, "and now let's look through the eye that still has a cataract." I could see, but the shining light was missing. "Those cataracts grew so slowly that I didn't realize how they were clouding my vision," I reflected. "How wonderful it is to see clearly again," I rejoiced. "I need to pause, look, and fully see while I still am able."

When challenged, Jesus returned again and again to Israel's first commandment: the Lord alone is God, and God alone is to be served (Mark 12:28-34). Be whole, complete, perfectly loving as is your heavenly Father (Matthew 5:48). People of God constantly open themselves to God's instructions and trust in the Lord's steadfast covenant love. Transcending ties of blood and family, true fellowship happens when we do the will of God. In amazing ways, the Spirit works within us so we become more compassionate and merciful, able to empathize with those who are in need or suffering, and do what we can to help. Grace and guidance happen together. Disciples who learn from and follow Jesus Christ become benediction people.

Ask and It Will Be Given Unto You

Jesus has a blessing and a promise that carry us through times when our calling, preaching, ministry, or missionary outreach is questioned. "Blessed are those who hunger and thirst for righteousness, for they will be filled" (Matthew 5:6). "Ask, and it will be given to you; search, and you will find" (Matthew 7:7). Monotheistic faith is rooted in the conviction that One who is both loving and just is in control of planet Earth and all life upon it. The biblical prophets and Jesus connected this conviction with the cosmic vision and assertion of liberty and justice for all, which Humboldt embodied. In the Scriptures, truth is a way of walking, where "truth" is discerned, lived out, and done in the guiding light of the Holy One. Seeing, living, and doing truth in kind, self-giving ways is being loyal and faithful to the steadfastly loving One who teaches us to pray. "Teach me your way, O LORD, that I may walk in your truth; give me an undivided heart to revere your name" (Psalm 86:11).

In the Jewish way of understanding, which shaped Christian Scriptures and the Koran, the heart is the seat of our will and thought. With undivided hearts, we can fear our Creator and loving Guide (the Hebrew word *yirah*, meaning fear, can be translated as "revere" and "be filled with awe," as well as "fear"). A person reading Psalm 86:11 and using a commentary on the Psalms that was translated from Hebrew to English would discover that key words such as *fear* or *truth* meant something different to the authors than to us. The very differences would be illuminating, beginning a process in which the Scripture questions the reader! Do

I, for instance, have the kind of undivided heart that, as Søren Kierkegaard once said, can will one thing?[14] If not, how can that happen to me?

Martin Buber said that we begin to be the whole person we were created to be by cleaving to the Lord.[15] When we cleave to the Lord, we begin to comprehend ourselves as a whole, and a mysterious process transforms and restores us. Conflicts with others are effects of conflict in our own soul, Buber continued, and as we think, speak, and act, we find our own self—not in the trivial ego of the egotistic person, but the deeper self of the person living in relation to the world. We choose to behave with personal integrity not only because it enriches and heals us but also because God's unconditional love flows through us to others. Filled with joy, delight, and kindness, we make peace with ourselves and then can make peace in the whole world.[16]

When I realized my pancreatic cancer could not be cured by medicine, I turned my life over to the Lord. Though I made that decision, not long after, I awoke in the middle of the night once again trying to control what was happening to me, worrying, "I'm going to die!" I asked the Lord to help me let go and let God. Soon I fell asleep, waking up in the morning in my right mind.

Turning one's whole life over—letting go and letting God—necessarily means regeneration, as in the Alcoholics Anonymous twelve-step program, where steps four through ten deal with doing a fearless searching of one's moral inventory. Why do we do an inventory? So that we begin to discern why we feel self-doubt, guilt, shame, anxiety, or fear. As we look deeply within, we discover we can forgive and make amends. Then, as we do so in loving ways that do not injure others and ourselves, we become more whole, coming to practice "praying only for the knowledge of [God's] will for us and the power to carry that out" (step eleven).[17]

When they learned I was dying, friends began praying for me. Since our bodies are created good to be temples of God, I asked the

Lord to help me do what I could do to take care of myself: exercising, doing physical therapy, and eating a diet with the goal of starving the cancer while feeding me. Continuing my daily walks and indoor exercises was not hard. At age eighty-nine, however, changing what I ate for breakfast, lunch, and dinner was a huge challenge. An integrative health specialist physician suggested that I change to a modified keto diet with organic meats and vegetables without herbicides, pesticides, and antibiotics.

New learning started out with unformed opinions, drawing on observations, experiences, and cultural traditions shaped during my lifetime (often in subconscious ways). As I let go and let God, I asked the Spirit of Wisdom to pour Her gifts of knowledge and understanding into me. I began to see changes I needed to make from a God-given perspective. The Lord energized gifts, abilities, and experiences I already had, and I began to feel more knowing relationally and intellectually, like stepping out of a dark place into warm, life-generating light.

My attitude toward my cancer changed. I stopped seeing it as an enemy and began to realize it was a part of me that was misguided by the pesticides, herbicides, and antibiotics in the food I ate—it was afflicted and confused. "Talk to it as you would a child," said my physical therapist. "Tell the little fellow to get back in balance with your body because he's going to take himself out prematurely at the same time as you die."

Two months later, I remained in the land of the living but had lost twenty pounds and felt tired all day. Was I overdoing my 100 percent dietary turn from death to life? My daughter, Beth, and Dr. Quinn, my oncologist, said, "You've got to eat more carbohydrates and increase the number of calories in your diet!" Their words hit hard—maybe I was starving myself. When we started measuring the weight of food I was eating, I discovered, indeed, that I was only eating half of the calories I needed to keep going.

You and I are finite, limited beings. By letting God handle how long I would live and when I died, the Holy Spirit's regenerating power freed me to do what was necessary to care for myself and unify myself for the sake of the living world—and that meant changing my entire diet at eighty-nine years old! I felt overwhelmed. It was like leaving home and moving to another country where I didn't know the language and everything tasted strange and unfamiliar. What did I eat for breakfast, lunch, and dinner? Could I discover desserts that tasted sweet and yet had no sugar?

"Owen, you're not in this alone," the Spirit seemed to be saying to me. "Ask your friends to help you find out what to eat and ways to cook tasty meals." Drawing on her early education as a nutritionist, a Kendal friend, Terry Wallace, discovered a recent book titled *Keto for Cancer* and bought a copy for me.[18] As a friend of many years whom I'd asked to stay with me for a while, Bill Cannon aided me in looking up meal suggestions on the internet and studied *Keto for Cancer* with me. We purchased two books with detailed meal suggestions.[19] "You have to learn to cook keto-friendly meals that taste good," Terry said. "Learning to change your diet comes from preparing food, as well as asking others to help you."

The Creator's light shines in and through the universe, "For with you is the fountain of life; in your light we see light" (Psalm 36:9). As we learn to live in God's light, our cups overflow (Psalm 23:5). We see a tree we've noticed a hundred times suddenly burning with green vitality and hear the sounds animals and people utter as they go about living. Safe, joyful, and delighted with what we see and hear, we know we are surrounded by friends on earth and friends above. Loved and accepted by the One who made us, our lives are now purpose-filled. As we follow Jesus and serve the Lord and our neighbors, old abilities are energized, and new gifts we never knew we had appear. When you or I decide to open to the light of God, we, too, shine, first like a tiny candle and then with brighter and brighter gleam.

Conclusion

When we seek and find, God's love shines in and through us. When we join the Lord in a lifesaving mission, he restores our losses and suffering. When we seek refuge under the shadow of the everlasting arms, we experience the Source of life who brought us into being and provides food and drink until we die. Then we see miracles happen every day, as the Spirit once again saves humans and animals alike. Let your light shine. Burn with the self-giving love of God, give off light and warmth, and in dark times shine like a star. Truth lights the way.

Notes

1. Messages from the Lord come from Genesis 12:1-4; Exodus 3–4; Psalm 36; Matthew 7:7-29; Romans 3:1-26; James 5:1-11; et al.
2. Andrea Wulf, *The Invention of Nature* (Vintage Books, 2015), 51.
3. Wulf, *The Invention of Nature*, 67.
4. Wulf, *The Invention of Nature*, 98–103.
5. Wulf, *The Invention of Nature*, 101.
6. Wulf, *The Invention of Nature*, 101.
7. Wulf, *The Invention of Nature*, 155.
8. Margaret Barker, *Creation: A Biblical Vision for the Environment* (T&T Clark, 2010), 9, 241–43.
9. James Muilenburg, in so many ways has shaped my life and ministry, yet he did reflect an overemphasis on history when he wrote, "Creation was the prologue to a particular history; reflection upon it is derivative from God's action in history. History is the primary area of the divine revealing, and the universe of nature is subservient to it. The heavenly bodies were created that man might live in God's created time and by the Word addressed to him." *The Way of Israel: Biblical Faith and Ethics* (Harper Brothers, 1961), 17–18.
10. Barker, *Creation*.
11. Barker, *Creation*, 50, 213–49.
12. Barker, *Creation*, esp. 248.
13. Douglas John Hall, *Imaging God: Dominion as Stewardship* (Eerdmans, 1986). Hall's work also helps us see and understand more clearly the definitions of faith as *assensus* (assent) and *fiducia* (trust). Each dimension of faith, whether assent to truth or trusting relationship, is subject to twisting and perversion when we turn away from God. Claims of infallibility are signs of faithlessness, since they make ultimate what is finite. Many arguments about light and truth would be resolved if we followed Calvin's teaching and turned our mirroring selves to the

light of God.

14. Søren Kierkegaard, *Purity of Heart Is to Will One Thing: Spiritual Preparation for the Feast of Confession*, translated with an introductory essay by Douglas V. Steere. New York: Harper & Bros., 1938.

15. Martin Buber, *The Way of Man: According to the Teachings of the Hasidim* (Routledge and Kegan Paul, 1950), 29–30.

16. Buber, *The Way of Man*, 33.

17. The Twelve Steps of Alcoholics Anonymous, accessed July 18, 2025, https://www.aa.org/sites/default/files/literature/The%20Twelve%20Steps%20of%20Alcoholics%20Anonymous%20-%20SMF-121.pdf.

18. Miriam Kalamian, *Keto for Cancer: Ketogenic Metabolic Therapy as a Targeted Nutritional Strategy* (Chelsea Green, 2017).

19. Domini Kemp and Patricia Daly, *The Ketogenic Kitchen: Low Carb. High Fat. Extraordinary Health* (Chelsea Green, 2016); and Dana Carpender, *200 Low-Carb High-Fat Recipes* (Fair Winds, 2015).

CHAPTER 3

Rescue the Perishing

Unfortunately, everybody messes up sometimes. You fall away from God and get lost. When you decide to hand yourself over to your Maker, as did John Newton, God pours gracious love into you as a gift! People are saved when they choose life and the God of the living. Lifting up animals and persons who are perishing revitalizes individuals, the congregations we join, our families, and our nation. God calls us, therefore, to be *anthropos* anglers, fishers of people who reach out with words and deeds of love and hope to those who are perishing (Deuteronomy 30:11-20; Mark 1:14-15).

Salvation Servants

In the 1980s, Jon Alston, a little boy of mixed racial parentage was growing up in Newark, New Jersey. If you lived in Newark then, you had every strike against you. Somebody, however, saw this boy's interest in music and invited him to join a choir. Jon loved music, studied, learned, and became a master singer and musician. Years later, seven responded to his invitation to join a children's choir in Chester, Pennsylvania, a city where people struggle to make a living. In July 2023, I attended a summer concert of the Chester Children's Choir, which now has 150 voices. The hall in Swarthmore College was packed. Jon led children from second grade to high school seniors in a powerful and delightful performance.

Offered a tenured position at Swarthmore College, Jon turned it down to devote full attention to the choir, which practices twice a week, once after school and once on Saturday, with an hour of music and an hour of math each time with professional teachers. Seeing a need for uplift through education, Jon founded a charter school in Chester, which now teaches students from kindergarten through twelfth grade. Graduates have been accepted at some of the best colleges and universities in America. Every fall Jon goes to each second-grade class in Chester and, one by one, asks boys and girls to be part of the children's choir, approaching them with humor and language on their level. Every child is created in God's image, and each has amazing gifts. Imagine what all of us might have missed had not somebody seen Jon Alston and invited him to join a choir.

Everybody gets lost sooner or later, including ministers of the gospel like me! In 1988 Evan Jones came into my office in the American Baptist Mission Center. I was struggling with what seemed like overwhelming difficulties in my mission work and marriage. Knowing Evan would keep what I shared confidential, I opened up to him.

"Owen," Evan said after hearing me out, "I counseled many as a military chaplain, and I have seen people make it through when they had trouble at work or when they had family trouble." After a pause, he continued. "But I haven't seen anyone make it through when they had work and family troubles at the same time!"

"My goodness," I thought, "I have both kinds of trouble, and they haven't taken me down. I must be doing okay!" Had Evan approached me with pity, I would not have been encouraged. He first listened and then challenged me to be the man I was in Christ. He lifted me up when I was going down.

As Evan and I grew to know each other better, I realized his life testified to the power of God's love in Christ. Growing up in a troubled family in a coal city with a declining economy, in his midteens, Evan was out on the street most nights. A Christian layman got to know this wild and struggling young man and saw in him

God's image. He reached out with caring words and deeds, and shared with Evan the good news that God loved him, and Christ died for him and was calling him to repent and live a new life. The young man listened, heard, was baptized, and eventually became a minister of Jesus Christ.

As a Baptist minister, army chaplain, husband and father, denominational leader, and regenerator of the Alaska Baptist Children's Home, Evan got up at daybreak and prayed for each person he might relate to that day. Our times of prayer still inspire me. "Owen," he would say, "don't forget your Welsh heritage. Read again *How Green Was My Valley* and keep your environmental justice concerns moving forward. Keep praying!"

One day we hear a call, a voice shrouded in mystery, saying, "Trust me, follow me, and serve as I served." From the time I was a child, I knew I was going to be a minister of Christ. As I grew up and prayed for direction, God provided answers. I never expected, though, that in 1970 I would see that the limits of nature were bringing to an end the progress and development of industrial societies. At that time, I decided that I would give myself to helping people move toward ecological wholeness and social justice at their points of intersection (eco-justice).

We are looking for a savior today—Jesus comes to find lost people and save us so we can live fully and wisely. To live we need food, clothes, clean water and clean air, a decent shelter, and good health care. The pursuit of happiness is shaped by living in a beautiful land, with friends and fellowship abounding, for games, humor, drama, music, and prayer. Liberty is necessary to pursue happiness, for human well-being depends on having a say in decisions that affect our well-being.

Turning to God means having faith that God has the power to care for you—no matter what happens, the Lord provides. Having faith in God means facing the realities outside and inside you with honesty and risking being in touch with your thoughts and feelings.

If you admit you need life-saving help, you will see what is coming toward you and receive the Spirit's power and guidance to deal with it. Believing in the Lord means being guided by Jesus' goals for ministry, to bring good news to the poor, proclaim release to the captives and recovery of sight to the blind, let the oppressed go free, and proclaim the Jubilee year of the Lord's favor—when debts are forgiven and everyone has the opportunity to make a new start (Isaiah 61:1-2; Luke 4:18). Believing in Jesus Christ means trusting the Lord to save you, learning and doing his teachings, and witnessing to Jesus Christ's life-saving love in what you do and say, indeed, living as a servant of the Servant of the Lord (Matthew 28:18-20).

Seductive voices also call us. When the Evil One takes hold of somebody willing to do anything to be rich, famous, and powerful, that person receives a compelling message: "Do you feel threatened, alone, lost? Follow me! Be a man! Your life, family, and country are in danger. Trust me. I'll see that you get work and live well again. Do what I tell you. Put your inferiors back in their place. Beat down those who took away your job, and our country will be number one again."

The American dream is threatened. Our economy is made from our ecology. Industrial and economic expansion has ecological limits. Climate change shows how fragile planet Earth is. Infinite growth of population, cities, and industries in a finite world is impossible. The frontier is gone.

Simultaneously, wealth flows from poor, working, and middle-class people to the tiny group at the top of the pyramid. The more money is concentrated at the top of the system, the less there is for everybody else. Working people struggle to make a living. From birth, you have been taught that anyone who works hard can succeed. Though you've learned to measure your worth by the money you earn and the pickup truck you buy, you feel deep inside, "I'm failing, and nobody cares about what's happening to me."

When you feel down and ready to give up, you'll be tempted to blame someone else for your troubles. You might start kicking your dog or try to beat up somebody in a bar. At the same time, you feel so bad about yourself, so alone, so lost, so despairing that you start looking for meaning and power outside yourself. Yet even as tempters beguile, in our hearts we know only the One who made us is the fountain of life. Pursuing material success is chasing a fading dream that cannot satisfy (Isaiah 55:2; Matthew 6:19). Desiring an ever-expansive standard of living threatens to destroy our minds and bodies, indeed our very souls. "For what will it profit them," said Jesus, "if they gain the whole world but forfeit their life?" (Matthew 16:26).

The Spirit right now is saying to you, *God don't make no junk.*

- You—yes, I mean you, are created in my own image.
- I know the American dream you spent your whole life preparing for is crumbling—of course you feel lost, alone, and afraid.
- My warm, healing light shines in and around you.
- You can be serene and live a fulfilling life right now where you are.
- A loving community of family and friends is waiting for you to come home.
- Turn off the superhighway to death—decide to live, now and forever.
- Choose life for yourself and your country, and I'll lead you to regenerate liberty and justice for all, starting with your family.

God calls us to be *anthropos* anglers who shine with loving light!

Fishing for Growth

I love rivers and streams. A lifetime of fishing began with my dad's bedtime story about fishing with another salesman on a Minnesota lake. A northern pike took Dad's daredevil lure—a fish so big, it began pulling the boat into deeper and deeper water. "Take us back," the man shouted, but Dad kept playing that fish as it moved away from shore. Suddenly the man pulled out his knife and cut the line. The big one got away—and did every time Dad told the tale!

When I was five, my dad took me to the Cambria, Wisconsin, millpond on opening day of fishing season. In the warm sunlight, I saw cane poles sticking out everywhere, their yellow color reflecting in the water. Dad gave me a pole, showed me how to thread the worm on the hook, swung the bait out into the water, and told me to pull when the cork went under. After several fruitless pulls, suddenly I felt something and pulled so hard the sunfish flew over our heads onto the bank. Dad then slid his hand over the fish to hold down its sharp fins as he unhooked it, first gently doing the same thing with my small hand. My fishing days had begun.

When Dad hooked me on fishing, I could not wait to get a big one like the one he lost! In the Midwest in those days, a boy became a man by learning to fish and hunt. Sport and providing food for the family were intertwined. As I grew older, I treasured times alone, silence broken only by birdcalls and the sound of water moving over riffles. When I became a teenager, cane poles gave way to a fly rod as I explored trout streams in the spring and then shifted to bass fishing with plugs and a casting rod in the summer. Part of growing up was learning to respect what was dangerous and discovering how to take care of myself. I took life-saving lessons at Rock Lake, walked carefully over slippery mud, and kept the treble hooks on the big lures away from my head!

Cast—retrieve, hour after hour, yet staying focused on the lure so that when a fish struck I was ready. When patience wore thin or I felt tired, I sat down and noticed all that was happening: glints of light reflecting from drops of water on tree branches, dragonflies darting up and down, a squirrel edging near the water and sipping a drink. From time to time, I became part of the flow of life, immersed yet intensely awake and aware. Respect, appreciation, and gratitude coursed up inside me.

Fishing changed me! Being in nature allowed me to see what human beings were doing to mess up the water. In high school I read in the daily newspaper that fish were dying because creamery waste was flushed into the river, using up the oxygen. The next time I crossed the bridge on my way to school, I looked at the creamery, and sure enough, the water was like milk below the pipe from which waste flowed. "They have no right to do that!" I exclaimed to myself. "It will kill the fish!" At that moment, a young fisherman became a conservationist.

I have been a fisher all my life. But when my mind and heart changed from catching and using to conserving, I was able to help make a difference. In Chester County, we built a vital stream conservation organization around people who loved to fish, felt they had taken a lot, and wanted to put something back. When Carl Dusinberre, a successful real estate developer, was in his late forties, his wife left him, and then a heart attack put him on total disability. He decided to take up trout fishing and oil painting, two interests his career had caused him to neglect. Carl then married a widow who had several children, and together they blended a new family. Before long, the "Dus" joined the Valley Forge chapter of Trout Unlimited, where his presence was like an elemental force of nature. Carl applied the lessons he had learned from his career and family life to saving Chester County streams.

"Hey, don't cut right down to the creek!" he would say to a young fellow with a Weedwacker trimming a yard, and then he would explain why a natural plant buffer kept stream banks from eroding. At a particularly discouraging chapter meeting, Carl would lift us up by telling a joke. He polished his writing skills with columns in *Banknotes*, our chapter newsletter, and everybody delighted in his witty family Christmas letter. His amusing and inspiring cartoons with George Washington looking over our shoulders provided the illustrations for *Living Waters: How to Save Your Local Stream*.[1]

Carl was a conservation evangelist. Woe to the hapless angler he met as he was fishing. "See this stream. You just caught a trout. If not for Trout Unlimited, there would be no fish here. Here's our brochure. Fill it in, join up, and come to our next meeting!"

Faced with a divorce, life-threatening health problems, and an end to his career, Carl could have let hard times take him down. Instead, he was grateful to be alive and thankful to contribute to making this country a better place to live. Carl D. chose life.

Fishing for People

In 1869 Fanny Crosby wrote a hymn that once echoed all over America:

> Rescue the perishing; care for the dying;
> Snatch them in pity from sin and the grave.
> Weep o'er the erring one; lift up the fallen;
> Tell them of Jesus, the Mighty to Save.
> Rescue the perishing; care for the dying.
> Jesus is merciful; Jesus will save.[2]

"Since all sinned and fall short of the glory of God," wrote the apostle Paul (Romans 3:23). By "the glory of God," he meant what we could have been if we had lived up to who we were created to be. The Bible says we are given life-saving words of hope and blessing that are to be spoken and taught to suffering people, starting with ourselves. "Beloved, let us love one another, because love is from God; everyone who loves is born of God and knows God. Whoever does not love does not know God, for God is love" (1 John 4:7-8). The Lord calls preachers to proclaim the gospel of God's love, for people need to hear these guiding words as we move into hard times.

My lifelong love of rescuing the perishing and fishing connected on a trip to Alaska. Before leaving, I read *Faces at the Bottom of the Well* by Derrick Bell.[3] Once again I was brought face-to-face with racism in North America and felt its destructive consequences. Our weeks in Alaska did not lift my despair over what I had read. As I fished the Kenai River, I saw stream banks eroded from the pounding of human feet. Beer cans, plastic bags, monofilament, and even discarded treble hooks used for snagging salmon littered the ground.

What does it mean when a species self-named *Homo sapiens* for its wisdom chooses to ignore human and ecological reality? What does it mean for a species marked by consciousness to have developed European imperial systems that used slave labor to devastate environments throughout North and South America, leaving in their trail ruined lands and impoverished peoples? We seem to continue from generation to generation as though we have learned nothing. How can we call ourselves *Homo sapiens* when we choose to live in ignorance, living as though the natural order can be used to draw out inexhaustible resources, aiming to be rich and acting as though the trees, fish, water, iron, and oil will last forever? Truly, as Dr. Seuss put it, we are "Once-lers."[4]

I woke early one morning with a song in my mind: "So high you can't get over it; so wide you can't get around it; so low you can't get under it, you've gotta come in through the door."

"This spiritual was born out of centuries of severe and demeaning oppression," I said to myself. "How is it that African Americans, oppressed so hard they could not stand, could produce such a song of hope and acceptance of limits?" Then I wondered, "What does this song mean for me? The ocean of racial injustice and ecological devastation is so vast that my little efforts are only an atom in this vast sea of need."

As the song ran through my mind, I reflected, "Our Lord called people who fished for a living to follow him. Suppose we were fishing with Jesus. What would it mean to be fishing for human beings? *Anthropos* angling, what a strange idea!" Fishing for people, however, is not a strange idea to a stream conservationist, because to save a creek from ruin, everything depends on finding somebody to organize an environmental movement. People who fish learn to be patient: "I know the fish are here. I know I caught them before, and I hope I will catch one this time." In Trout Unlimited's work, I have seen those who love to fish tolerate uncertainty and continue to move forward with "impossible goals," despite the modern development's destructiveness, starting to conserve, preserve, and restore local streams and their watersheds.

Leonard Ball, our Alaskan guide the day Irene and I fished for king salmon on the Kenai River, helped me better understand why Jesus called fishermen to follow him when he gave us instructions before we boarded his boat: "I know this river and will take you over the fish. To fish well from my boat, you have to be a team. Everything depends on the one with the rod. You have to feel the fish, strike, hook, and play it. If you make a mistake, you'll probably lose it. Lots of times you'll lose the fish whether you make a mistake or not. When there is a fish on, everybody must do their part. One person puts up the net and stows the rod so that nobody gets hooked, while the other concentrates on catching the fish. I will move the boat up and down the river, follow the fish, and as patiently as I can, work the boat until the fish may be netted. Keep your sense of humor—everything goes better when you stay a little detached."

Everything Peter, Andrew, James, and John learned in their years of commercial fishing was applied to *anthropos* angling. With Jesus as their guide, they would become ministers of God's kingdom. They heard him proclaim the saving benefits of God's rule that we now call the Beatitudes (Matthew 5:1-12). They saw him heal the blind, sick, and lame and, when he was criticized for it, show that the very touch of God was doing this life-saving work (Luke 11:20). They were shocked to see him break the prejudices of his day by talking with women as equals (including many as his disciples), taking little children on his knee and blessing them, and healing a Gentile woman's baby. The disciples followed Jesus to Jerusalem, fell away when he was arrested and killed, went back to fishing one last time, and were gently brought back by the risen Lord to their calling as they sat around a campfire eating fish he had cooked. As they shared that meal together, Jesus forgave Peter for denying him three times and commissioned Peter to be an *anthropos* angler who would feed Jesus' sheep (John 21:15-19).

The day is here when we, like Jon Alston and Carl Dusinberre, will have to choose between a way of life that builds up streams and people or our desire to pursue an ever-expanding material standard of living. If we decide to work for liberty and ecological justice for all, we and our beloved land will experience a new birth of freedom. The gospel of God revealed in Jesus Christ is good news, calling us to choose life and not death. The Holy Spirit asks us to turn from the way that leads to death, face ourselves, become truly free, love all our neighbors as ourselves, and become God's *anthropos* anglers. *Anthropos* anglers reach out to the perishing together!

Fishing Together

"Lead us not into temptation," prayed Jesus, "but deliver us from evil." The Scriptures tell us that hard times are to be received as times of testing. Even the worst disasters that may fall upon oneself, family, land, and nation are not to be feared. Neither are such times of temptation to be desired. They bring out the best and the worst in us. Fred Krueger, head of the National Religious Coalition for Creation Care, shared with me,

> For Christians, the cross is the key to facing not only death but also the wilderness. The cross banishes fear and hesitation as it represents the faith in life that allows us to confront every challenge of the wild and tells us that our lives

> are not confined to this body, but life is greater and tied into the timelessness of God and creation. The stern nature of the cross reminds us that beyond this body, life continues and expands into other dimensions. In this way, wilderness becomes a teacher about abundant life.[5]

Christians believe Jesus Christ embodied the love of God, died on the cross to save us from sin, was raised from the dead, and transforms us to follow the way of life he walked (1 Corinthians 1:23-24). Gospel preachers, Protestant and Roman Catholic, have shaped American life from its beginnings. For more than thirty years, I served in the American Baptist Home Mission Societies. Baptist home and foreign missions were started to call people on the expanding frontier and in other nations to turn to Jesus Christ, baptize disciples, establish churches, and minister to people of special need. Along with evangelism went Christian civilizing, teaching believers to learn and practice Jesus' teachings.

Each generation of Baptists was informed and challenged by prophets. When the men who ran the mission societies refused to appoint women, Baptist women formed their own mission societies! Baptist abolitionists called church members to free their slaves and end slavery. After the Second World War, Baptist seminaries opened their doors to Black students, like Martin Luther King Jr., and both home mission and educational ministry societies broke color line prejudices in appointments, as in selecting Rev. Jitsuo Morikawa as secretary of evangelism in 1956.

Coming into Baptist life as a Methodist minister, I met people who were indeed saved by the living Christ, as, for instance, Evan Jones. When Dr. Ernestine Galloway asked Jones to guide Baptist mission work in Alaska, he brought Black and white churches together in the Greatland Baptist Association. How much good happened because a Christian lay evangelist reached out to a young man on the streets?

Nations change. Unprecedented economic expansion undercuts itself. Young people see a future with no promise, no hope. On May 24, 2022, an eighteen-year-old boy in Uvalde, Texas, shot and killed nineteen school students and two adults before he was killed by police. Such suicidal mass murders remind us that as civilized restraints dissolve, lost human beings do terrible things to others and destroy their own lives. The Spirit of the living God calls evangelists to proclaim the whole gospel of Jesus Christ to people who need to know, "I am somebody. There is hope for me. God is calling me to use my gifts to make this world a better place to live."

You may be saying, "All right, Owen, but when I preach that Jesus incarnates God's love and calls people to give their lives to him, why don't people listen? Our congregation is losing members. Young people drop out and don't return. I don't understand what's happening."

The question of why people aren't responding to our salvation message has vexed me since I was a teenager studying to become a minister. When in England in 1965, I pursued this question at the Oxford University Bodleian Library. I found out that although for the preceding fifty years people in the United States had been dropping away from religion, it was around 1910 when the British middle classes began to fall away from the churches. Each year, denominational membership tended to drop (roughly paralleling the decline of the Liberal Party), a decline that has not yet been arrested. Quakers, for instance, in their generative years, may have claimed the allegiance of a third of the British people but now have fewer than ten thousand active members.[6]

Yet every day new lives are born who, with care and protection, will someday grow to be a forest of hope. When people are freed from evil, they move from death to life. Being saved and saving, freed and freeing, loved and loving cannot be divided. Nor can God's life-giving power be restricted to our own species, class, gender, religion, or nation. Acts of cosmic significance happen when a Black woman refuses to sit in the back of a bus and a minister takes up a world-transforming mission. When Rosa Parks walked and Martin Luther King preached, the word again rang out throughout the world. Mohandas K. Gandhi allowed his life to be an experiment with truth, and the British Empire lost its power over India.

Loving service leads us into the presence of the living God. Democratic Pennsylvania state senator Andy Dinniman (served 2006–2020) often brought Chester County, Pennsylvania, religious leaders together to share with others about their charity work. When I walked in the door at a recent gathering, I was amazed. The Assembly of God's big social hall was packed with several hundred people. Around the room were tables telling about services for Chester County's poor. Pentecostals and Roman Catholics, Methodists and Lutherans, Jews and Muslims all came together united around the Lord's directive to feed the hungry and help the needy.

The evening concluded with worship. We sang and prayed together. Then two elderly rabbis invited us to come to the center aisle. Slowly, carefully, they unrolled a scroll of the Hebrew Scriptures that had been preserved by burial and survived the Holocaust, though most of the congregation's members had been murdered. "Don't be afraid to touch the scroll," said the rabbi. "It's worn, and a piece may break off in your hand, but don't worry. We will all touch these words of God gently together, and as we pray, God will strengthen us to love our neighbors as ourselves."

As we touched that sacred scroll preserved by such sacrifice, the Spirit of the living God moved in us. Since God's commandments to love God and our neighbors as ourselves could draw us together in works of charity, cannot the same thing happen with reaching out to those who are perishing? Suppose leaders of the children of Abraham came together to set up tables and share what they are doing to call American souls to choose life, "so that you and your descendants may live" (Deuteronomy 30:19).

"Jews, Christians, Muslims, Buddhists, and other folks of different faiths coming together to do something like a Billy Graham crusade!" I can hear someone say, "You've got to be kidding—or a little bit crazy." Maybe so but maybe not. Imagine when times get hard, as in the Great Depression, and truly mad men and women are preaching hate on the internet, TV, and the streets. Choices for life or death will be made that will shape the future. Divided, we are weak. United, our voices will be heard. The gracious and merciful One will show us religious folks the way.

Billy Graham's campaigns centered on metropolitan areas, and Protestants of all varieties joined together to hold evangelistic services, seeking the conversion of individuals through a message, songs of praise, and an invitation to give their lives to Jesus Christ. In an interfaith effort, we come together, using the loving protocol, and lift up a common witness to our conviction that the Creator of life is Lord of the cosmos. Each faith group speaks its own message of hope and invitation. We Christians witness to our conviction that the Creator of life and Lord of the cosmos took on human flesh, became incarnate, was born of the Virgin Mary, worked as a carpenter with his dad, and learned to read and write, as did every Jewish son. When he grew up, he proclaimed the good news of the kingdom of God right here on earth. Jesus taught us the Sermon on the Mount, which he directed all disciples to follow. His parables, such as the good Samaritan and the loving father and prodigal son, as well as the Lord's Prayer, show us how we enter God's kingdom on earth. Near the end of his time on earth, Jesus went with his disciples to Jerusalem to make clear that the kingdom of God began with the nations and was intended to bring them into the way of loving peace. In the garden of Gethsemane, he was betrayed and arraigned before Pontius Pilate and religious leaders. He was tortured, crucified, and died on the cross. After three days, the Lord raised him from the dead. Now Jesus Christ sits at the right hand of God the Father Almighty and will come to judge the nations at the time the Lord chooses.

God is not a bitter judge hating fallen human beings. Every one of us has gifts, strengths, and insights. The Lord says to use your gifts to make a difference for good (1 Corinthians 12–13). Without a vision, the people will perish (Proverbs 29:18). How will they hear without a preacher? (Romans 10:14-18). The message of God's redeeming love goes to the roots of the ecology-justice crisis. We who preach the good news of a loving God have an awesome task. "Call lost people to repent and use their time, money, power, and position for the common good," says the Lord.

Conclusion

How much poorer our lives would be if someone had not invited Jon Alston to join a choir or if a Christian layman had not reached out to Evan Jones with the gospel. When we go home, we learn new ways we are being led through the ecology/justice crises to better days ahead. How much weaker our local conservation movement would be if Carl Dusinberre had not decided to choose life? How less interdependent would Chester County religious leaders be if Senator Andy Dinniman had not brought them together? Modern *anthropos* anglers hear God's call, leave commercial nets, and follow the Holy Spirit into desolate prison, urban jungle, suburban desert, ruined farmland, and devastated wilderness to call human beings, one by one, to enter God's new future of love and eco-justice for all.

Notes

1. Owen D. Owens, *Living Waters: How to Save Your Local Stream* (Rutgers University Press, 1993).

2. Fanny J. Crosby, "Rescue the Perishing" (1869, public domain).

3. Derrick Bell, *Faces at the Bottom of the Well: The Permanence of Racism* (Basic Books, 2018).

4. From Dr. Suess, *The Lorax* (Random House Books for Young Readers, 1971).

5. Phone conversation with Fred Krueger, January 2017.

6. For penetrating studies of what was happening, see Benjamin Seebohm Rowntree, *Poverty: A Study of Town Life* (Macmillan, 1901); and *English Life and Leisure: A Social Study* (Longman, Green and Co., 1951). In Russia the Communist movement was anti-religious, and then in Nazi Germany mass murders of Jewish people were grounded ideologically in ways that challenged faith in Jesus Christ and living by his teachings; both countries historically were Christian.

CHAPTER 4

Homeland Healing

God's creation of human beings reflects constant love and care. Made in the image of God, formed from the ground, we return to living soil when we die. As we turned from the tree of life and grasped the fruit of the tree of the knowledge of good and evil, we multiplied without limit, subdued the earth, and dominated the living creatures. When, through God's atoning grace, we are restored, we have access again to the tree of life, and our Lord walks with us as we resume our task of tilling and keeping the garden which is planet Earth.

Regenerative Community: How Eco-Just Peace Comes on Earth

The human and ecological problems we face call for a new vision of a regenerative community. Without a vision, the people perish—actually unravel (Proverbs 29:18). Our Western civilization did not keep the Greek word for home, *oikia* (the origin of the suffix *eco-*), at the center of our thinking. As Jeffrey Sachs, economic theorist at Columbia University, reminds us,

> *Ecos* is the root of *ecumenical*—the household in the entire world, the total of humanity; it is also the root of *economia*, economy and household; and of *eco-logia*, where organisms live in the contexts of their homes. To understand why we are in deep crisis, Aristotle in his *Politics*, reminded us that *economia*, household management of wealth, has as its end purpose to reach well- being, the supreme good; to achieve this purpose requires *promesis*,

> building virtues so that we handle wealth with prudence and generosity—wealth must be guided by virtue.[1]

If the idols of our era sell us to think of our continuing care community as a money-making industry, managed like a top-down corporation, we will stop caring for people, land, and water.[2]

As a regenerative community emerges, we are guided by elemental values. A century ago, Albert Schweitzer was in a boat edging through a herd of hippopotamuses when he realized the future of Western civilization depended on reverence for life. When we are reverent, we respect the right of every living being to exist, and we begin to live interdependently, looking not only to our own interests but also to the interests of other persons and creatures. As we grow in reverence and interdependence, stewardship of all given to our care becomes our practice. As we restore, we leave the part of the planet we touch a more beautiful and just place to live.

There is a great deal more to life than "wise use." Who wants to be married to a partner who wisely uses you? True relationships are grounded in respect and appreciation for the identity and worth of one's beloved and of oneself. When we go out into the living world of nature with our ears and eyes wide open, we appreciate every living being we meet. As we rediscover our interdependence with the world of nature, caring emerges naturally, as when a mother holds for the first time the tiny baby to which she just gave birth. "Life is beautiful, wonderful!" she feels. "I want to feed and care for my child."

Jared Diamond, in his book *Collapse*, lists the serious problems we face:

1. We are destroying natural habitats or converting them to human-made habitats, such as cities and villages, farmlands and pastures, roads, and golf courses.

2. The great majority of fisheries have already collapsed or are in steep decline, but wild foods, especially fish and shellfish, contribute a large fraction of the protein consumed by humans.

3. A significant fraction of wild species, populations, and genetic diversity has already been lost, and at present rates, much of what remains will be lost within the next half century.

4. Farmland soils used for growing crops are being carried away by water and wind erosion at rates between ten and forty times the rates of soil formation, and between five hundred and ten thousand times the soil erosion on forested land.

5. Fossil fuels are the major energy source used by industrial nations. Further reserves will be deeper underground, dirtier, increasingly expensive to extract or process, and have higher environmental costs.

6. Most of the world's fresh water in rivers and lakes is already being used for irrigation and domestic and industrial water; freshwater aquifers are being depleted at rates faster than replenishment; mountain glaciers, which in Asia supply a billion people with water, are rapidly melting.

7. Perhaps half of earth's photosynthetic capacity is being used or wasted by humans. Less and less is being left to support the growth of natural plant communities such as forests.

8. Toxic chemicals pour out into air, water, and land: insecticides, pesticides, herbicides, mercury and other metals, fire-retardant chemicals, refrigerator coolants, detergents, plastics, nuclear waste, and more.

9. Alien species are transferred to a place where they are not native, often wreaking havoc on native species.

10. Human activities produce gases that escape into the atmosphere, damaging the protective ozone layer. These gases act as greenhouse gases, absorbing sunlight and thereby leading to global warming.

11. The world's human population is growing; more people require more food, space, water, energy, and other resources.

12. As the rest of the world adopts American living standards, more resources are consumed and wastes produced, increasing per-capita impact progressively.[3]

Faced with these ecology-justice problems, if we continue to devote ourselves to progress through infinite growth, civilization cannot hold together. We face a dark future. Pursuing profit, comfort, and pleasure, nations of users, takers, and consumers do not respond decisively to Diamond's twelve eco-justice problems. Sooner or later, the stock market will crash, as it did in 1929 and 2008. Once again those with a passion for social change will take to the streets. La Follette–style progressives, socialists, Marxists, anarchists like the Tea Party, and fascists backed by the gun lobby will argue that their ways will solve our problems. Preachers of hate will blame a defenseless minority and the protection of the environment for causing economic distress, pontificating that the evil way is the right way, for after all, "greed is good." Wars over increasingly scarce water and land will devastate life. Then will come two or three hurricanes in one year, along with crushing droughts, followed by floods of environmental refugees. Change will come, for good or evil.

Freed to Live and Love

Climate change is the presenting issue pressing down upon us, calling for radical changes in the way we think, relate, spend and earn money, and live together. Ignoring what is happening, then denying climate change is real, and finally facing climate scorching in despair all allow us to escape from deciding to do what we can to make things better. Lester Brown, founder of Worldwatch, has outlined a comprehensive plan of jobs for protecting and restoring the earth's beauty and its prodigious variety of life—a necessary goal. He reminds us that if civilization is to survive, not only must we eradicate poverty and stabilize population, but we must also restore the earth, protecting and restoring forests, conserving and rebuilding soils, regenerating fisheries, protecting plant and animal diversity, and planting trees to sequester carbon. Restoring the chain of life requires providing food sources for insects, resident and migrating birds, and the four-legged animals. The light of truth guides us to respect and care for the community of life with understanding, compassion, and love in ways that embody social justice.[4]

Brown also reminds us to have hope: We face an extraordinary challenge, but there is much to be upbeat about. All the problems we face can be dealt with by using existing technologies. Almost everything we need to do to move the world economy back onto an environmentally sustainable path has already been done in one or more countries. In the United States during the Second World War, new jobs were created, old ones were phased out, and gasoline and food were rationed because we knew our lives were at risk. Here are some steps we can take today:

- We can and must eradicate poverty and stabilize the population by providing universal basic education, family planning services for all, and better health care, and by reducing farm subsidies and debt.
- We can restore the earth by protecting and restoring forests, conserving and rebuilding soils, regenerating fisheries, protecting plant and animal diversity, and planting trees to sequester carbon.
- We can feed eight billion people well by rethinking land productivity, raising water productivity, producing protein more efficiently, and moving down the food chain.
- We can design cities for people, including redesigning urban transport, reducing urban water use, farming in the city, and upgrading squatter settlements.
- We can turn to renewable energy, harness the wind, manufacture wind-powered electric cars and vehicles, install solar cells and collectors, draw energy from the earth, turn to plant-based sources of energy, and use river, tidal, and wave power.

The head of Rodale Press, Robert Rodale, was testing plans for regenerative community development before his untimely death. In local experimental projects, two or three community leaders came together, traced the boundaries of their local ecosystem, examined the economic potential for long-term ecologically sustainable development, and generated a plan for action. In Europe, leaders are rewilding agribusiness land, returning to sustainable farming practices in balance with nature. In South and Central America, logged and worn-out land is being rejuvenated with syntropic agriculture, restoring rain and cloud forests in ways that are food productive. *The Biggest Little Farm* documentary, recently shown at Kendal Crosslands Community, explores such a project in the greater Los Angeles region.[5]

The fear of the Lord is the beginning of wisdom, say the Hebrew and Christian Scriptures. This teaching expresses the Creator's intent to restore the bonds of the creation covenant described in Genesis 1. Human beings are created in the image of God. Our souls and bodies, all we are, are made by the Holy One to be "very good" (Genesis 1:31). When we choose to eat the fruit of the tree of the knowledge of good and evil, we fall away from our Maker, each other, and the living world of nature (Genesis 1–11). When separated from our Source, we do what appears necessary to be secure, prosperous, and recognized, no matter who gets hurt. Then what we make, use, and control takes power over us.[6]

"If the Source of life on earth is steadfastly loving and kind," you may ask, "why is fearing the Lord the beginning of wisdom?" Fear of the Lord is the starting point of wisdom because we come into life, live briefly, and die. Living, growing, aging, and dying go together.[7] When light shines on us, it dissolves the dark, protective armor we vainly spend years making. Who does not feel awe when light shines? Within the senses of smallness, limits, and creatureliness lies the elemental fear of being plunged, unprotected, into the forces that brought our planet and all life into being.

In Hebrew and Christian Scriptures, the heart is the decision-making, willing center of our being. Ordinal light—kind, loving, personal—shines around and inside us, but we fear that light.

"What would happen to me," we wonder, "if I let go and let God?" When we experience awesome fear of the Lord, we receive the other gifts of the Spirit—knowledge, understanding, power, discernment, counsel, and wisdom—and at once start to love God and our neighbors as ourselves.

In Genesis 2, human beings are made from living earth. In Hebrew the name *Adam* means human and seems to be related to *adamah,* which means ground or earth. We can think of ourselves as *adam* from *adamah,* formed from the ground, returning to the soil when we die: "The biblical story says that the creation was entrusted to Adam *before he sinned* and lost his glory, and Adam losing his glory was reflected in the degradation of the earth. This the key to the biblical story: the degradation of the earth is the direct result of the status of human beings; what they are/believe themselves to be determines what the earth becomes."[8]

God's creation of human beings reflects our Creator's very character, constantly loving and caring, now, in the past, into the future, from beginning to end (alpha to omega). Made in the image of God, you and I are able to love and care, as Jesus did when he loved his enemies. When sinful Adams multiplied without limit, subdued the earth, and dominated the living creatures, the result was—and is—disaster. When, through God's atoning grace, the *adamah* is restored, we have access again to the tree of life, and our Savior walks with us as we resume our task of tilling and keeping the garden.[9]

Rocks and mountains, springs and rivers, grasses and forests, insects, birds, reptiles, mammals—all creatures want to be brought into holiness. Wholeness happens when we humans open ourselves to redeeming light and shine with that light, reclothed with robes of glory.

Unmerited suffering brings us together. Jews and Muslims are children of Israel, as are we Christians. Elie Wiesel, in *Four Hasidic Masters and Their Struggle Against Melancholy,* showed how deeply we are joined together.[10] One great master was the Seer of Lublin, who gave his followers exuberance, joy, fervor, celebration, enthusiasm, and ecstasy, overcoming their experiences of melancholy, sadness, and despair. Yet he wrestled with his own melancholy:

> Most Hasidim came to the Rebbe to unburden themselves of their misery and anxieties. And the Rebbe listened—listened well. And empathized. And identified. Well, how long can one go on hearing tales of woe and tears? Of hungry children and persecuted fathers? Week after week, day after day, hour after hour the Rebbe would listen to the misfortunes of his people in the various small communities ruled mostly by wicked landowners. How could he stay immune? One morning he had to wake up with a broken heart.[11]

Rebbe Yaakov-Yitzhak possessed a powerful vision. In early youth, he asked the Lord to take away his burdening awareness of present and future. "He saw too much, too far," says Wiesel, "but his plea was not answered."[12] Shortly before he died, he called his disciples together for a great celebration. Joyful singing and dancing went on late into the night. Unnoticed, the Seer of Lublin slipped out of the room into his study. When they missed him, his followers went to his room and found it empty. Hours passed as they searched. Suddenly, close to the house, they heard a weak moaning. Reb Shmuel of Karov held his master's head as they carried him. He heard the Seer softly intoning ancient lamentations, repeating, "And the abyss calls for another abyss."[13]

> Could it also be that in a sudden flash of fear the Seer had a glimpse of the distant future when night would descend upon the Jewish people and particularly upon its most compassionate and generous children—those of the Hasidic community? Was that why he strayed outside? To wait under the somber sky, abandoned and shattered, to

> wait and wait through several generations, if necessary for other victims of other catastrophes?[14]

Children of Abraham, along with people of all faiths, know that the unlimited growth and development engineered by human beings leads us toward an abyss. As with the Seer of Lublin, those who see and pray and love feel sadness, melancholy, and despair. Jews, Muslims, and Christians seek God in different ways—yet we experience being found and freed by the Lord from hurting ourselves and others in the exact circumstances of our lives. Our leaders know that to deal with the ecology-justice crises threatening life on earth, our Maker calls persons from all faith traditions to join together.

Dietrich Bonhoeffer, facing suffering and death, observed that by uniting science, technology, and bureaucracy, modern human beings seem capable of meeting everything except themselves! God copes with human nature at our worst and best through Jesus, who inexplicably is able to exist for others. In the brief time before he was executed, Bonhoeffer wrote that the good news of God in Jesus Christ comes to us in a message of *metanoia*, repentance, allowing us to be caught up in Christ's way, loving the created world and those living in it.[15] Jesus exists for others, suffers as a result, and in that suffering, takes humanity's burdens upon himself. One lives, therefore, not by judging others self-righteously, but by grace through faith. Then God pours out on us the sevenfold gifts of the Spirit of Wisdom—fear of the Lord, knowledge, understanding, power, counsel, discernment, and wisdom. The living God is with us in the concrete circumstances of life in this century—in joy, suffering, and everyday life. Out of the truth that comes by trusting in God's righteous love comes freedom.

Homeland Healing

We can join the Lord as peace agents on earth. John Newton made a good living as a captain of a slave ship. Slavery was the economic engine that gave the British Empire power. Few questioned their support of it. One account of Newton's change of heart says, "Newton was aboard a ship one night when a violent storm broke out. Moments after he left the deck, the crewman who had taken his place was swept overboard. Although he manned the vessel for the remainder of the tempest, he later commented that, throughout the tumult, he realized his helplessness and concluded that only the grace of God could save him. Prodded by what he had read in [Thomas à] Kempis['s *Imitation of Christ*], Newton took the first—albeit small—step toward accepting religion. In the words of his hymn, this incident marked 'the hour I first believed.'"[16]

Later Newton reflected on his twenty years as a slave ship captain, and his conscience was troubled as he remembered the twenty thousand persons whom he condemned to terrible lives, and those he had killed, throwing them overboard in a chain because he did not have enough food to sustain them all as they were carried to America. He couldn't remember any of their faces and didn't know any of their names. When he wrote the now-famous hymn "Amazing Grace," he applied specifically one phrase to himself: "That saved a wretch like me!"

One day Newton was visited by William Wilberforce, a speaker in Parliament. Wilberforce told Newton he was discouraged by the responses to calls to end slavery in the empire and wondered if it was important for him to keep going. Newton strongly encouraged him and shared the deep burden he carried. He reminded Wilberforce to persist, trusting that Parliament would listen at the right time.[17]

Lincoln Ended US Slavery, but Racism Persists

> Oh, we were always honorable—Robert Lee, Jackson, Albert Sidney Johnson, A. P. Hill—but we served venal men and a vile enterprise. How many lives would have been spared had we not lent ourselves to the defense of a repellent cause like slavery?[18]

American Baptist churches show us ways to move forward in overcoming racism. The American Baptist Home Mission Society (ABHMS) was established in New York City in 1832 to preach the gospel, establish churches, and support ministry among the unchurched and destitute. By 1836, 150 home missionaries were at work in fourteen states, two territories, and two provinces. Women wanted to help with God's work, but the American Baptist Foreign and Home Mission Societies refused to appoint single women as missionaries at that time. In response the Women's Baptist Home Mission Society (WBHMS), based in Chicago, was founded in 1877, and Joanna P. Moore became its first fully commissioned missionary. Another women's society, the Woman's American Baptist Foreign Mission Society (WABHMS) was also founded in 1877 in Boston "to extend the kingdom of God among the women and children of America." Over the next century, these missionaries accomplished great things:

- Founded twenty-seven institutions of higher education for Freed People after the Civil War
- Sent an envoy to Washington to work for treaties favorable to Native Americans
- Opened a Baptist Missionary Training School in Chicago
- Appointed missionaries to serve in Michigan, New York, Puerto Rico, Alaska, and Arizona
- Ministered to Japanese Americans in internment camps during World War II
- Worked with Church World Service, following World War II, to relocate thousands of refugees to safe homes[19]

In the twentieth century, the three home mission societies united in the service of the American Baptist Convention, later known as the American Baptist Churches USA. Building upon many decades of such inclusive home mission work, in 1956 Theron Chastain appointed Jitsuo Morikawa to one of the denomination's most powerful positions in the Division of Evangelism. This white American Baptist leader's risk released floods of energy. The New Testament tells us that the body of Christ includes everyone whom our Lord calls, and that when many members function as one body, the Spirit activates us to do amazing things. Starting in 1968, Morikawa led ABHMS's governing board and staff in strategic planning. Then, in 1972 the board adopted a goal of structural change of institutions toward ecological wholeness and social justice at their points of intersection. American Baptist leader Richard Jones coined a new term, *eco-justice*, showing that social justice and ecological wholeness are inseparable, joined together by values of reverence for life, interdependence with life, and stewardship of life.

Morikawa observed,

> Ecological wholeness and social justice can become handles by which to hook into history and participate in the shaping of the future. They appear to be among the most enduring issues which speak to the depths of human existence and the meaning of salvation. Salvation, the goal of the gospel of Jesus Christ, is that new reality, love of God and love of neighbor, so that, in the words of Richard Niebuhr, the ultimate purpose of God for the world "is the increase among men and women of the love of God and neighbor." But the ecological issue raises the biblical insight that salvation involves not only our relation to God and neighbor but also our relation to nature: our love for it, our respect for it, and our proper treatment and stewardship of the land and the earth.[20]

The 1972 United Nations Stockholm Conference on the Environment provided an opportunity to test the adequacy of the ecology/justice goal. Gary Herbertson, a Methodist minister who had been working on ecology concerns with churches in Southern California, proposed to me that religious leaders convene at the Stockholm Conference on the Environment. More than thirty responded to our invitation, coming to Stockholm and meeting at a cathedral each day, then spreading out to cover the happenings. Listening to addresses and talking with participants from all over the world, I became convinced that the board's ranking of trends was not an ephemeral effect of Earth Day 1970, but instead an accurate expression of the forces shaping the planet.[21]

Healing and My Hometown

Fort Atkinson, Wisconsin, my hometown, could be a place where homeland healing starts. Hugh Highsmith's research and writing reveal truths in Fort Atkinson's bloody history that we were all dimly aware of in high school. Without truth, no possibilities for change for the better appear. Imagine that you are a teacher in the Fort school system. Restricted by state and federal instructions geared to teaching to the test, how do you communicate what you've learned to students in high school? Nothing you try seems to work. Then you read about how, once at Fort, a debate club dealt with important topics. Students were assigned either to support a position or to oppose it.

Imagine that you announce an initial meeting for interested students. Only two show up, but you give them a copy of Highsmith's book, ask them to read it and to prepare for a debate. One is assigned to support Highsmith's writing about what happened to native people. The other is assigned to take the opposite position. They come in rather tentatively at first, then more excitedly as the debate builds. Before the next scheduled meeting, the invitation goes out to other students to participate, and upon learning that the first debate was fun and illuminating, several more turn up.

You decide it is time to invite other schools in the area, maybe Edgerton, Stoughton, or Jefferson, to put together a team and come over to Fort Atkinson and have a debate. Stoughton says,

"Yes, we will send a team—you pick the debate topic," and you assign Highsmith's book. Several parents show up at the debate to support their students, and not surprisingly, one or two are fascinated by the topic and begin to feel led to do something to make things better. Young business leaders begin to explore ways the community might move forward progressively, and they include native people in the planning. Suddenly you see a community response that may promote homeland healing.

Imagining a Healing Ministry

Suppose you are a minister in the community. You study about peace on earth, and how structural change of institutions toward ecological wholeness and social justice together are essential to carefully produce, prepare, and deliver messages for your church people. They listen politely, but it seems like you get no response. Then a member of the church suggests that maybe it's time you should explore putting solar panels on your roof. "Sounds like a good idea," you respond, not knowing whether anything will come of it. The church member, however, gets in touch with several other members, and they do a little research and come up with a plan as to what can be done and how the congregation might pay for it. The board approves the idea, and soon the roof is covered with solar panels, providing energy. Then the original committee says people are putting in solar collection batteries and selling back the power at peak through the utility company. "Let's do it," says the board, and now there's solar-powered backup in case a big storm knocks out power, and some of the cost of installation is being paid by selling back power to the utility.

Encouraged by what is happening, you invite community leaders from the diverse religious faiths to come for a meeting to explore how you might have a public dialogue, sharing stories about helping your community's less fortunate with their needs. Tentatively, at first, each faith leader prays in their deepest soul language. When they discover that they are listened to with respect, they feel free to share their thoughts and feelings with one another.

At a subsequent meeting, as people feel comfortable with one another, someone suggests that you bring together leaders from each faith group to share what members are doing to help, heal, and find housing for people at the bottom. Having begun with a discouraging situation, you see that your small efforts are leading to major changes in the life of the community.

Imagine you are a conservationist who would love to see the Rock River and its tributaries restored and its water run clear and cool again, the way it once was. Yet it seems like you're the only person interested. When you share your thoughts, you get no response. You decide to prepare a talk with audiovisuals, using beautiful pictures taken along the Rock River. Whenever you have an opportunity to speak and show your pictures, you do it.

Somebody comes up to you after a presentation and says, "Maybe if you and I work together, we'll get something going to restore this river and its watershed." The new volunteer is an organizer, and after getting her feet under her, she begins to make connections with native peoples. They discuss how land might be restored that was once their traditional camping and hunting grounds. Together they plan to bring bison, elk, and wolves back to Wisconsin—provided land can be secured to allow the big mammals, which once shaped the ecosystem, to return. Then the big corn-to-oil factory closes its production plant because federal subsidies to this intensely polluting industry have ended. Suddenly land becomes available—large tracts of it. Sauk and Winnebago tribes seek out and gain access to the considerable funding necessary to acquire enough land to establish traditional camping, hunting, and gardening grounds on traditional land. Then tribes take the lead in bringing back bison, elk, and their predators to Wisconsin. These animals once played a key part in ecosystem maintenance. People came from all over to see the big animals, and communities that have lost their economic base find new opportunities in eco-tourism. What started small and was often discouraging resulted in massive changes toward homeland renewal.

One woman read in Larry Gibson's biography about how he used food and music at family events with outside speakers to form a family foundation that saved Kayford Mountain from destruction by Massey Coal's mountaintop removal. She thought, "Maybe it's time, with all the things that are happening to restore the land and water, to hold a big celebration at the old Masonic building on Rock River. People will bring food, and we'll serve good bratwurst produced locally. We'll have several local singing groups and one or two outstanding speakers about institutional change toward ecological wholeness and social justice."

With a positive response from the community, a gathering is scheduled for a summer day. Bill and Kitty of Café Carpé secure singers and musical groups to set a positive tone for the day. When the day comes, the venue is so crowded that many struggle to get in, but hosts find a place. The celebration inspires, uplifts, and takes the whole regenerative community movement forward.

Years later a municipal government leader announces that maybe it's time to prepare a plan. He announces, "A lot is happening in Fort that's moving us forward, and we need a plan for the future to move forward as a progressive city." Of course, community leaders who have been struggling for this goal for years say, "What a good idea." Movement forward is enough reward for years of organizing.

Conclusion

Imagine that Hasidic master Yaakov-Yitzak is speaking to us. He might say, "Stop fighting with each other. Look at what suffering you've caused among your own sisters and brothers, and now your people are killing nature." We have seen ways that institutional change toward ecological wholeness and social justice has and can happen in America. Let us change our ways while there's still time. We can start by learning to respect and love each other, and by doing what we can to restore life on earth. We need to begin right where we live. The Lord is good and will lead us through.

Notes

1. From author's notes on Jeffrey Sachs, address to the Greening Attica Conference, Athens, Greece, June 2018.

2. Owen D. Owens, *Living Waters: How to Save Your Local Stream* (Rutgers University Press, 1993), 4.

3. Jared Diamond, "Collapse: The Dozen Most Serious Environmental Problems and What We Can Do About Them," *Skeptic* [Altadena, CA] 11, no. 3 (2005): 36+. *Gale Academic OneFile* (accessed August 4, 2025). https://link.gale.com/apps/doc/A130930465/AONE?u=anon~281664e6&sid=googleScholar&xid=13cd2f6c.

4. Lester R. Brown, *Plan B 3.0: Mobilizing to Save Civilization* (Norton, 2008), 3–19.

5. *The Biggest Little Farm*, directed by John Chester (LD Entertainment, 2018).

6. Margaret Barker, *Creation: A Biblical Vision for the Environment* (T&T Clark, 2010), passim.

7. See Andreas Weber, *The Biology of Wonder* (New Society, 2016), ch. 3.

8. Barker, *Creation*, 194–95, emphasis original.

9. Genesis 2:15; see also Leviticus 19–26 (the Holiness Code); Deuteronomy 32:43; Romans 8:19-20; and Revelation 2:7. See Barker, *Creation*, 195.

10. Elie Wiesel, *Four Hasidic Masters and Their Struggle Against Melancholy* (University of Notre Dame Press, 1978).

11. Wiesel, *Four Hasidic Masters*, 91.

12. Wiesel, *Four Hasidic Masters*, 72.

13. Wiesel, *Four Hasidic Masters*, 64.

14. Wiesel, *Four Hasidic Masters*, 94.

15. As referenced in a letter of Dietrich Bonhoeffer to his friend, Eberhard Bethage, written from Tegel Prison, dated 21 July 1944.

16. "The Creation of "'Amazing Grace,'" Library of Congress, accessed July 21, 2025, https://www.loc.gov/collections/amazing-grace/articles-and-essays/creation-of-amazing-grace/.

17. Karen J. Ristuccia, "Mentoring a Georgian-Era Daniel: John Newton and William Wilberforce," The Washington Institute for Faith, Vocation, and Culture, accessed July 21, 2025, https://washingtoninst.org/mentoring-a-georgian-era-daniel-john-newton-and-william-wilberforce/.

18. James Lee Burke, *In the Electric Mist with Confederate Dead* (Pocket Books, 1993), 432. Cited in Allen C. Cuelzo, *Robert E. Lee: A Life* (Knopf, 2021), endorsement pages. Note that this is a fictional quote in a nonfiction book.

19. David Charles Laubach, *American Baptist Home Mission Roots 1824–2010,* American Baptist Home Mission Societies, accessed July 21, 2025, https://ccl.abhms.org/products/digital_downloads/american-baptist-home-mission-roots.

20. Jitsuo Morikawa, "Theological Meaning of Ecojustice Through Institutional Change," *Foundations: A Baptist Journal of History and Theology* (American Baptist Historical Society) 17, no. 2 (April–June 1974): 100.

21. Renewal of community and change of consciousness were included as ways to move toward structural change of institutions. For articles on the ecology-justice goal, see *Foundations: A Baptist Journal of History and Theology* (American Baptist Historical Society) 17, no. 2 (April–June 1974).

CHAPTER 5

Invest in the Future of God's Creation

A vision of creation justice leads us to a way we long to live. Restoring nations and natural life go together. Change for the better in America and all the world's nations is necessary and possible.

Leading the Way: Cities Regenerated to Be More Life-Sustaining

It is possible to build cities that are just, ecologically restorative, and participatory. During the Middle Ages, Muslim Spain built cities that tolerated Jews and Christians, as well as fostered learning, medicine, the arts, and commerce. Simultaneously, Roman Catholic monasteries worked with local people to improve farming practices, grind grain using water mills, and foster learning that flowered in the medieval universities and was foundational for industrial civilization. Puritans fleeing persecution in England adapted European agricultural systems to New England, building productive farms, prosperous towns, and growing cities. Individuals could participate in this new order through self-governing congregations and town meetings. They formed schools to teach everyone to read, write, and figure. Humans can solve problems for many when we collaborate to solve those problems.

Today climate change forces millions to become refugees. The Bible tells us to welcome the stranger. Muslims, Jews, and Christians would not be here today if someone had not welcomed refugees like Moses, Joseph, and Mary with the baby Jesus. Rather than furthering human-caused environmental catastrophes, we can invest in building model communities that welcome refugees and restore their local ecosystem.

Eco-justice crises like climate change not only close the doors to economic growth in the old exploitative, consumerist way but also open new doors to a more just and ecologically whole way of life. We can engage refugees—working with local residents—in building just, participative, ecologically regenerative communities in the United States. This experimental community would be chartered with the goal of restoring its local ecosystem.

Imagine this nation of immigrants inviting climate change refugees to opportunities to rebuild communities in which solar energy generates power and batteries store it, hydroponics produces food in the buildings, and rainfall collectors provide and recycle water. As people unite to build safe, beautiful places to live, imagine those communities paying for research and jobs to preserve, protect, and restore their regional ecosystems. Vanishing fossil fuel–based jobs will be forgotten as productive work, compensated with decent wages, plans and restores future communities. It is time to propose to communities starved for job-creating investments, like Chester or Coatesville, Pennsylvania, that they plan to rebuild a community for the future.

Ground-laying precedents provide clues for moving forward. Americans again and again have worked hard to improve their lives. Throughout the country, abandoned city lots are revitalized by residents into gardens to grow food where they live. With volunteer and sweat equity labor, Habitat for Humanity builds housing for those who are homeless or living in degrading conditions and creates a generative funding model by which modest monthly payments seed new projects. The New York City Water Department, recognizing the necessity of restoring the watersheds and rivers that provided clean water for millions, began investing in stream and watershed restoration, which indeed helped revitalize regional ecosystems. China created vast new cities that house millions of people, more than there are refugees in the world now. The technology exists to build cities that collect and recycle their own water, raise food hydroponically, and provide all the solar power needed.

Money follows mission. James Rouse, who participated in the Church of the Savior in Washington, DC, took to heart that Jesus Christ directs us to be like a city that shines with the compassionate, powerful light of God. He felt called to form a corporation to build a new town that became Columbia, Maryland, which he intended would embody universal love. Fifty years later, we see a diverse community, where in the days of the COVID-19 lockdown, people walked the trails through the greenways and parks. We remember how Rouse broke centuries of racial prejudice that prevented Black people from getting a mortgage and buying a home in white-controlled areas.[1]

Johns Hopkins Hospital, located in Baltimore's inner city, decided not to move away from impoverished neighborhoods dragged down by crime but instead to stay, employ, educate, promote excellent community workers, and invest in upgrading community housing. Today when people from all over the world come to Johns Hopkins, they are welcomed and assisted by people who have skin colors like theirs and speak their languages. By deciding to stay, invest, and serve, both the hospital and the city moved forward.

Communities that are more ecologically whole and socially just are possible. All that is needed is someone with the experience, skills, and expertise to form nonprofit corporations like Resources for Human Development (RHD) or Habitat for Humanity and get grants to build communities chartered for ecosystem restoration. Of course, doing so would require a diverse and competent staff, people who know the cultures and speak the languages of those who learn and work together to build communities for the future.

In 1970 Bert Wolfson, who was getting started as a lawyer, received a call from a friend who had been named head of mental health in Montgomery County, Pennsylvania. Mental health facilities were being closed, and seven catchment areas were identified to provide help for people who were moved out of the facilities. The Pennsylvania legislature voted for the funds. When his friend asked, "Will you set up a program for the lower main line?" Bert agreed to help.

Mental health patients needed care, so Bert formed a nonprofit company, Resources for Human Development (RHD). He organized a counseling service in Lower Merion. The organization started one group home after another, and soon Resources for Human Development had considerable expertise. Part of the grants received were used to form an ongoing nonprofit corporation with a board of directors. The Great Society programs helped support their development, enabling them to hire people who could gain trust in the community, and eventually RHD became an economic driver that provided good salaries and opportunities while helping neighbors in need.[2]

Seeking Structural Change of Nations and Their Cities Toward Creation Justice

Writing in 1974, Jitsuo Morikawa, prophet to the twenty-first century, warned,

> For the last four hundred years we have lived with the unquestioned assumption of an infinitely exploitable planet, of endless frontiers and exhaustless resources. So, fueled by a scientific/technological capability and a driving work ethic, we have plundered and ravished the earth with little thought of recycling its resources for future generations. If the present trends in pollution, exhaustion of resources, and population growth continue, knowledgeable scientists speculate that there will be a planetary catastrophe by the year 2020.[3]

Almost fifty years later, Morikawa's words resound, not leaving us in despair, but calling us to change our ways and move in a new direction:

> Where the worldview of infinite frontiers prevails, the ethics of individualism, independence, aggressive initiative, growth, and production are rewarded. In the new world of spaceship earth, the global village, the critical values essential to human existence may be the ethics of interdependence, instant communication, collaboration and participation, equity and equilibrium, freedom within social control, humility and meekness, so that the marks of human greatness will be radically altered. Self-willed, ego-driven, power-hungry leadership may become relegated into obsolescence and be replaced by one whose passion and obsession is equity and justice for all.[4]

Speaking to Christian churches, Morikawa tells us to have hope:

> But how can the church with its limited resources confront vast "principalities and powers"—corporations, governments, universities, communication industries—to deal with such vast issues as ecology and justice? The greatest asset the church possesses is an unconquerable faith that God the Creator of heaven and earth and the Shaper of human history is at work transforming this world toward the new creation. Our legacy of hope in God's triumphant mission is our greatest human asset: "I can do all things through him who strengthens me."[5]

Climate change is the presenting issue that presses upon us, calling for radical changes in the way we think, relate, spend and earn money, and live together. We human beings are burning so much fossil fuel that the carbon emitted is heating the whole planet. Instead of ignoring, denying, or despairing about what's going down, we can respond to climate change in ways that deepen our life together. If the idols of our era encourage us to think of our cities and country as a money-making industry, managed like a top-down corporation, we will stop caring for people, land, and water.[6]

By investing in the future we long for, we continue the precious legacy of being caring communities. Science and religion press us to invest in the kind of future we want—and decide to act now while time remains. If we never forget that a kind and caring Spirit leads us to decide to put this spirit in practice every day as we relate to each other and our developed and forested lands, we will find that seemingly impossible challenges open the door to amazing new opportunities.

The Religious Coalition for Creation Care, which I co-chair with Rabbi Warren Stone, in April 2019, issued the "Religious Declaration of Unprecedented Human Emergency" regarding climate change:

> We are committed to responding to the cry of the Earth and the cry of the poor. The harsh and often deadly impacts of climate change increasingly weigh upon the human spirit. Therefore, we call upon elected officials, faith communities, and the public-at-large to combat climate change at the scale and pace this emergency requires. We demand that policy-makers work together to reach the science-based climate goals of the IPCC to cut greenhouse gas emissions to at least 50 percent below 2010 levels by 2030. We also urge policy-makers to work together to ensure a just transition that protects the safety, health, and dignity of low-income and historically under-served communities. We look forward to the spiritual, health, and

economic benefits of living more simply, gently, and lovingly on God's good Earth.

Shortly before his untimely death, Robert Rodale, whom I mentioned earlier, told me that he picked the term "regenerative community" because it meant generating anew, reviving, recreating, and being reborn spiritually. From years of experience with organic gardening and farming, he saw local communities drawing a living from their regional ecosystem in ways that protected, preserved, and restored it. So, he tested plans for regenerative community development in local experimental projects. Two or three community leaders were brought together, traced their local ecosystem's boundaries, looked at long-term ecologically sustainable development's potential, and generated a plan for action.

Investing in the future we long for is possible and necessary. For many years, Jane Goodall, who pioneered the study of chimpanzees at Gombe, has been speaking to people all over the world. Many contributed to the Jane Goodall Institute (JGI), which she founded in 1977, seeing that unless people suffering in desperate poverty received help, they could not participate in saving chimpanzees and restoring their forests. In 1994 JGI began a new approach to conservation called Tacare. A team of seven local Tanzanians went into the twelve villages around Gombe and asked people what JGI could do to help. People wanted to grow more food and have better clinics and schools, so that's where Tacare started, not only doing what they could but also working with the Tanzanian government.[7]

Because they started with people right where they lived, listened to them, and acted on their concerns, people came to trust them. Gradually they then built a program including tree planting, protecting water sources, and setting up microcredit banks. In 2021 the Tacare program is in over a hundred villages throughout the range of the two thousand chimpanzees still living in their forest homes.[8] When we invest in the future we want to live in, amazing changes for the better will happen.

We move in the right direction when we begin to think and act in ways that lead to God's future kingdom of eco-just peace on earth. There is more to life than "wise use." Who wants to be married to a partner who wisely uses you up? True relationships are grounded in respect and appreciation for the identity and worth of one's beloved (not how much money one can make by using them). When we go into the living world with our ears and eyes wide open, we appreciate every living being we meet. As we rediscover our interdependence with nature, caring emerges naturally, just like mothers holding their newborn babies for the first time. "Life is beautiful, wonderful! I want to feed and care for my child," the new mother thinks.

A worldwide circle of love and an interdependent fellowship encompass planet Earth and all who live upon it. When we step off the ladder of self-advancement at others' expense, we enter a community that always has room for one more, for the circle of love, as the universe is constantly expanding. Just and loving treatment of the living world, including humanity, is guided by the Source of life who made us from the dust of the earth and redeems us to be good stewards who heal, help, free, protect, preserve, and restore—leaving this planet a more beautiful and just place to live.

Philosophers and theologians tell us that our desires to be more loved and loving are foundational, whereas dominating and exploitive styles of life destroy others and ourselves! People like John Muir, Mohandas Gandhi, Martin Luther King Jr., and Jane Goodall came to think and behave in ways that regenerated human and natural life. Ordinary people have changed direction and have become more reverent, interdependent, and stewardly persons of integrity. But are we too old to do much of anything? Late Kendal resident Peggy Brick would say, "You may be 'up in years' but you can still learn, teach, give, and speak out."

We at Kendal Crosslands Communities can create a regenerative community plan in which residents, the governing board, staff, and administration participate in making decisions about our common life and individual well-being. A caring community helps us see constructive ways to respond to the challenges of climate change as we reposition our living space and renovate our medical center. As we open ourselves to the light of God shining in every person, the elemental human values of our Quaker founders open a way forward.

Dr. Hans Joachim Schellenhuber, head of Germany's Potsdam Institute for Climate Impact, called on the world's nations to cut their carbon emissions by half in this decade:

- The amount of carbon in the atmosphere correlates directly with global temperature.
- Human beings have interrupted the global ice age cycle with looming risks. Recent scientific findings show that a temperature drop of 3.5 degrees centigrade caused past ice ages; one degree centigrade, therefore, is a large increase; if fossil fuel energy use continues to increase, by 2050 global temperature will go up by 8 degrees centigrade.
- Disastrous consequences multiply as global temperatures increase. Sea level rise threatens 1.5 billion people; hot and humid areas in South and Central America, Asia, and Africa will be uninhabitable without air conditioning; persistent droughts will cause widespread famine (estimated 30 percent rainfall decline in Greece); wars over control of water and land will intensify destruction of human beings and vulnerable species.
- If we want to achieve rapid decarbonization, we must confront our human ambition to get ahead and consume more than others; moving toward simpler, less-consuming lifestyles pales in comparison to the catastrophic changes that will fall upon us should we do nothing.

- Rapid decarbonization is necessary, with the goal of halving carbon emissions every decade. If we start in 2020, changes will be easier to manage by individuals, societies, and ecosystems.[9]

We Invest in the Future We Long to Live in When We Restore Nature

We inventive, industrious human beings have been unraveling the life systems on our planetary home, unmaking creation. The morning before Archbishop Bartholomew's 2018 Green Attica conference started, members of the Religious Coalition on Creation Care climbed Mars Hill, where the apostle Paul preached to the Athenians. We had to be careful because the limestone rocks were worn slippery-smooth by the generations who climbed before us. After a prayer time for the earth and each person in our circle, I looked out over the vast city of Athens, glistening white in the noonday sun. Not far away, blue ocean was visible. Over the patches of green forest that had been preserved, wispy fragments of clouds floated. Suddenly I realized that four thousand years ago, before logging had left bare, eroding slopes, and sheep and goats had eaten every tree shoot, the sun would have been shining dimly through clouds of water vapor transpired by the great forests, seeding summer thunderstorms.

Across our planet, remnant forests are being logged, chipped, and turned into agri-business fields. Generations of logging and plowing up prairies have created agri-business plantations that are almost entirely dependent on fossil fuel power. Herbicides, pesticides, and chemical fertilizers produce grains and soybeans for the world food market, emitting immense amounts of carbon into the atmosphere. Soils are eroding, losing their carbon-fixing powers, and water and air are being poisoned. Birds, animals, insects, and soil bacteria species show drastic declines, and many are going extinct. Slaves have been replaced by fossil fuel–driven machines, but land is still taken from Indigenous people, and ecosystems are collapsing. Owners may profit, but masses of people struggle to earn enough to survive. Our green suburban lawns are one with agri-business fields in being biological deserts. Even trees in national parks are burning as climate-scorching heat desiccates the land.

We are caught, trapped in a mindset alienated from nature. We wake up in our cottage, walk or ride to something happening indoors, eat in the café, drive to a supermarket, eat in the dining room, and attend the evening program or go home and watch TV—we seldom go outdoors. In this urban, technological, industrial society, when someone sees natural places, they start figuring out how to build on them to make money. When we human beings fall away from using our power to protect, preserve, and restore life-giving ecosystems on which we are absolutely dependent, we unravel, and so does everything we touch![10]

When we go outside and open the book of nature, we begin to see with new eyes. When I'm feeling down and hopeless, I take a walk on the Woods Trail through a grove of huge trees. I look up, following the immense trunks to where blue sky shines through the green branches. Walking around a decaying nurse log, I see that out of death and decay spring up ferns and tiny trees. As I come out of the Big Woods, I feel awe—these trees have lived longer than I, somehow escaping storms and loggers to touch the sky. New hope surges in me because I have seen the trees and am once again part of a green, diverse, beautiful, living forest.

In Western civilization, two words shape our understanding of the living world—*nature* and *creation*. The word *nature* comes from the Latin *natura*—that which is born, produced, and has an essential character, substance. The word *creation* comes from the first chapter of the Bible, which reports how the Creator spoke in the beginning and made all that is, declaring creation to be good.

The earth's ecological systems make life possible. Rivers, oceans, glaciers, forests, prairies, and tundra are all interconnected. Green chlorophyll in these life systems absorbs carbon dioxide and emits oxygen. From tiny ocean algae to immense redwoods, plants shape the earth's atmosphere and provide breathable air. When rain falls, its force is broken by the forest canopy, and water evaporates from leaves and branches. When you walk in the woods after a rain, you get wet from water dripping down on you, and the spongy forest floor absorbs almost every bit, allowing infiltration that revitalizes the springs that feed the rivers. In Chester County, Pennsylvania, where I live, transpiration from leaves and needles is so great that there is no summertime groundwater recharge. Transpiration creates clouds, giving birth to more rainfall. The air we breathe, water we drink, food we eat, even our very bodies and minds come from the great life systems that mother and father the living world and cradle the life of each child.

Both modern science and religion see the planet we live on as life-generating, constantly changing, and volatile. Human beings are one with nature in that we, too, are life-generating, constantly changing, and have volatile powers that can be as great as active volcanoes. Who would ever have thought that people could change the whole planet's atmosphere or cover the earth with vast cities, roads, and agri-business plantations?

Restoring nature is a key that opens the door to the future. Nature is alive, and every living being seeks to grow and extend life. Going solar is a necessary step toward healing the planet. Restoring nature means working with a degraded ecosystem to help it become healthy again. My wife, Irene, and I were at the Rio de Janeiro Environmental Summit in 1992, where we heard David Brower, founder of Friends of the Earth, share in his workshop that the goal of the summit was changed from nature's restoration to sustainability. He felt this was a serious error, because sustainability is a concept that may mean sustaining nature or sustaining our market-driven industrial society's lifestyle. The concept of sustainability, he argued, does not raise the hard questions posed by restoration.

When we at Kendal Crosslands Communities want to regenerate our Big Woods, for instance, we must go back to learn what Penn's Woods once was like. We must discover how the Lenape people and other tribes managed the forests, face what Euro-Americans have done to Penn's Woods, learn tested restoration possibilities, and then do what we can to help a degraded forest return to full life. To restore nature, we need all the help we can get. How do we human beings bring a natural system, such as a forest, back to fully productive beauty, life, and order? We need scientists who can help us understand and deal with diseases and insects that have been introduced here and are threatening to wipe out the ash trees. We need community organizers to challenge us to do what we can, no matter how old we are. We need inspiring spiritual leaders to encourage hope, for no matter how dark the future seems, the truth's guiding light shines.

Change to a green, life-filled natural land usually starts small. Kendal resident FM Mooberry offered a lesson for when we feel old, tired, and discouraged. She was a woman who saw what was happening and decided to do something right where she lived and worked. She started a movement toward a better world ahead. When replanting a degraded patch of land at the Brandywine Conservancy, she learned so much about the critical importance of native plants that she became an expert in the field. When she and her husband, Dave, moved to Kendal, they removed invasive plants from their cottage garden and planted striking native perennials and shrubs—their garden became a showcase. The Mooberrys educated us by having Doug Tallamy speak on his book *Bringing Nature Home.*[11] Highly visible, beautiful, and innovative natural areas make Kendal Crosslands Communities a leader among continuing care communities.

The Kendal community began to replant their forest starting in 2010. For years Kendal residents and staff have been bringing nature home. Pioneering restoration projects are ongoing here at

Kendal Crosslands Communities. We are not starting from scratch. As Dave Mooberry, back in 2010, learned more and more about how we human beings were unraveling nature, he discovered kindred spirits in the Trails Team, as Sid Berry and he found out that grounds manager Mark Swick had similar convictions. As they sweated together, clearing invasive ailanthus trees and multiflora rose from around Spear Pond, residents could soon see the striking ruins of the Harlan House, which was completed in 1705.

Fran Beer, with a faithful team, pulled out smothering invasives so that little holly shoots might become the beautiful grove it is today. Barbara Hallowell may not have succeeded in her request to have leaves remain on the ground as far as the drip line of trees, but staff began to put leaves around the base of trees—a step in the right direction. Dick Lighty, with his trusty lopper, cut vines off struggling trees at Coniston—today you can see straight trunks reaching for the sky, joined by the many trees that grounds staff and residents have planted.

Organic gardeners have been raising healthy food at our fenced vegetable plots. Not only have we been eating poison-free, tasty, fresh lettuce, tomatoes, and many other vegetables, but the garden soils sequester carbon and get healthier each year. We also send a lot of produce to food banks.

Starting in 2010, the Kendal Trails Team, working with grounds staff, planted native trees and shrubs in the Harlan Glen Pilot Project. Two oaks are now over fifteen feet high, and each spring native azalea blossoms fill the air with fragrance. Dave Mooberry prevailed upon the developer to seed with native meadow plants what has become the Stormwater Native Plant Meadows, and when the developer seemed unable to proceed, he bought the seeds himself. In 2014, Chotty Sprenkle, a Chester County Soil and Water Conservation staff person, saw these meadows and commended Kendal for being far ahead of most development projects.

Because the results of planting trees take decades to become apparent, the administration has to make a long-term investment in the human and financial resources to revitalize the natural lands. As the inheritors of Penn's Woods, future generations will realize the benefit of our efforts to initiate rejuvenation of the Big Woods.

Here are some of the next steps forward in bringing nature home, revitalizing the chain of life in Kendal Crosslands Communities:

- Use scientific knowledge and technical abilities to regenerate our part of Penn's Woods, putting ourselves in ecologically sustainable balance with the forests and meadows[12]
- Reestablish species of Penn's Woods in our arboretum and forests, and native plants in our meadows[13]
- Replace European cool-season grasses with native grasses and flowering forbs in our landscape[14]
- Reeducate our aesthetic senses to appreciate beauty in its creative, life-sustaining forms
- Find tested ways to infiltrate, transpire, and evaporate rainfall and sewage system effluent that put us in better balance with the water cycle

Listening to each other and acting on insights shared opens a way forward. As residents worked with administration and staff, we continued a dialogical tradition begun in the early days of Kendal Crosslands Communities when residents had a say in all decision-making. The director did not attend Kendal Resident Association meetings because he wanted full expression of concerns and knew that if he were present, some might not say what they thought. Participation in governing board meetings by residents was expected. As we move forward, it is critically important to deepen our life together as caring communities, not only with creatures of the living world that surrounds us, but also with our human relationships. To build our positive history and overcome our weaknesses, residents need to participate in decisions that affect our well-being.

All too often things break down because we don't get along with each other. By patiently listening, waiting in silence for a little while to reflect, and then sharing thoughts and concerns, we surface feelings of fear, anxiety, and hurts experienced in ways that deepen understanding. Some who did not know any Quakers learned to practice listening and sharing through human relations and organizational development training. When Dave Mooberry and grounds director Mark Swick proposed turning the golf course lawn near Harlan Glen into a native plant meadow, Harry Hammond brought together residents whose cottages bordered on that lawn with a Quaker-like process. People asked questions about Dave and Mark's proposal and raised concerns. Then they went home, reflected, talked, and came back with suggestions, as did Mark and Dave. Eventually we shaped plans that became our beautiful, life-generating native plant meadow that absorbs stormwater like a sponge.

Organizing and supporting movements to invest in the future we want to live in can make a big difference. When he retired as head of the Pennsylvania Fish and Boat Commission a few years ago, noted conservationist Ralph Abele said,

> One person with enough stubbornness can dig in his heels and say, "This much and no more." Beware of the cause that you choose for this kind of stubbornness, because you will surely prevail! There are great causes to be followed, and victory always starts with one person hanging on by her teeth and saying, "I will never give in." All the greed and shortsightedness of the exploiters and developers—and that includes people in state and federal governments—will not prevail if that one individual rises up and says, "Why should we put up with this?" I insist that if one

> is stubborn enough—unmovable, unchangeable—that person can and will prevail.[15]

Conclusion

Writing during World War II, Abraham Heschel, a Jewish Bible scholar who escaped the Holocaust at the last moment, called us to make this world an altar for God:

> There can be no neutrality. Either we are ministers of the sacred or slaves of evil. Let the blasphemy of our time not become an eternal scandal. Let future generations not loathe us for having failed to preserve what prophets and saints, martyrs and scholars have created in thousands of years. The Fascists have shown that they are great in evil. Let us reveal that we can be as great in goodness. We will survive if we are as fine and sacrificial in our homes and offices, in our Congress and clubs as our soldiers are on the fields of battle.[16]

We come from nature, live with all that is out there, and return to the earth when we die. It is time to get back in balance with the living world of nature, time to invest in the kind of future we want for our children and grandchildren. Residents and staff working together help Kendal Crosslands Communities become greener and more biodiverse and beautiful. On a beautiful October day in 2019, each child in our early learning center planted a tree along Bennett's Run. Assisted by grandparental residents who gingerly went down on their knees, each child wrote his or her name on a tag and put it on the tree they had planted. Each tree—each child—is a sign of hope.

Notes

1. Jimmy Stamp, "James W. Rouse's Legacy of Better Living Through Design," *Smithsonian,* April 23, 2014, https://www.smithsonianmag.com/history/james-w-rouses-legacy-better-living-through-design-180951187/.

2. "Mission & History," Resources for Human Development, accessed July 21, 2025, https://www.rhd.org/about-us/mission-history/.

3. Jitsuo Morikawa, "Theological Meaning of Ecojustice Through Institutional Change," *Foundations: A Baptist Journal of History and Theology* (American Baptist Historical Society) 17, no. 2 (April–June 1974): 101.

4. Morikawa, 101.

5. Morikawa,103.

6. Owen D. Owens, *Living Waters: How to Save Your Local Stream* (Rutgers University Press, 1993), 4.

7. David Gadsden, "Tacare: How a Global Conservation Movement Started with Community-Created Maps," *Esri Blog*, November 21, 2022, https://www.esri.com/about/newsroom/blog/goodall-tacare-human-wildlife-relationship.

8. Jane Goodall and Douglas Abrams, *The Book of Hope: A Survival Guide for Trying Times* (Celadon, 2021), 97–103.

9. From notes taken by author during an address by Hans Joachim Schellenhuber, Greener Attica Symposium, Athens, Greece, June 2018.

10. Edward O. Wilson, *The Creation: An Appeal to Save Life on Earth* (Norton, 2006), 7. "Ecosystems and species can be saved only by understanding the unique value of each species in turn, and by persuading the people who have dominion over them to be their stewards" (92).

11. Douglas W. Tallamy, *Bringing Nature Home: How You Can Sustain Wildlife with Native Plants*, updated and expanded ed. (Timber, 2009).

12. Travis Beck, *Principles of Ecological Landscape Design* (Island, 2013); Leslie Jones Sauer, *The Once and Future Forest: A Guide to Forest Restoration Strategies* (Island, 1998).

13. See Ben Goldfarb, *Eager: The Surprising, Secret Life of Beavers and Why They Matter* (Chelsea Green, 2018).

14. Douglas W. Tallamy, *Nature's Best Hope: A New Approach to Conservation That Starts in Your Yard* (Timber, 2019).

15. In his last article in the *Pennsylvania Angler*, May 1987, Ralph Abele, director of the Pennsylvania Fish and Boat Commission, preached the need for a conservation ethic, not an easy message to get across in a throwaway society.

16. Abraham Heschel, *Moral Grandeur and Spiritual Audacity*, ed. Susannah Heschel (Farrar, Straus and Giroux, 1996), 212.

Section 2
Restore the Earth and Ourselves

CHAPTER 6

Turn to Me and Live

Loving light shines. Inspired by the Spirit's life-saving power, the Lord calls us to proclaim a hopeful message to each person caught in the storms of life. We can hear the welcoming call of our Creator saying, *Come home to the One who made and loves you. Come home!* We start by learning to be *benediction people*, extending to others the blessings God has poured out on us. Then comes the promise the Creator makes: "Turn to me and be saved" (Isaiah 45:22). When someone hears and turns onto the narrow way of life, we join the delight of our Savior and invite, welcome, and include each one in our circle.

Becoming Benediction People:
Blessing the Earth and Humanity

"For with you is the fountain of life," exclaimed the psalmist. "In your light we see light" (Psalm 36:9). God is love—*agape*—personal, unconditional, overwhelmingly self-giving love. As Christians, we see God's light shining in the Father, Jesus Christ, and the Holy Spirit. The Spirit of God, Wisdom, calls us into being, is with us, and is in us. In the Hebrew and Christian Scriptures, Wisdom is the mother of the angels and many human children, including Christians.[1] She (the gender of the Hebrew word *hochmah*, translated as "wisdom," is feminine) births, feeds, gives drink, cleanses, sings, teaches, protects, and guides, as animal and human mothers do with their babies. Though we turn away from her tree of life, wandering as lost souls in the darkness, her light shines brightly, calling us home, where blessings abound. The Holy Spirit never gives up on us, for we are her children.

Wisdom in Benedictions

When religious leaders are present at family gatherings and community meetings, they are asked to bless the food or close the event with a benediction. How many times have I been ready to give an important message to a meeting, only to have the leader ask, "Owen, would you say the blessing before the meal?" When the founder of Sustainable Delaware Valley Consultations, Ernest Cohen, called and asked me to give the closing benediction, and I agreed to do so, I had no idea that a memory lapse would bless me beyond measure.

After a refreshing weekend at home, the Monday after the consultation, I looked at my calendar and realized I forgot to go to the Sustainable Delaware Valley Consultation and give the benediction! I'd broken my promise and let Ernest Cohen down. Remembering how Christians oppressed Jews, I reluctantly picked up the phone and called Ernest, and he answered. "Ernest, I'm really sorry I forgot to come and give the benediction," I confessed.

"That's okay, Owen," he responded, "you can come next year." I felt a sigh of relief—Ernest forgave me! Then he continued, "Please come and join us at our next Seder meal."

Ernest's Seder invitation was written on my heart as well as my calendar. No way was I going to forget it! When I arrived at his home, he welcomed me. Joined by family members, we ate and prayed together, remembering the formative event in our common history as Jews and Christians when the Hebrew people were delivered from slavery in Egypt. A few weeks later, Ernest set up a time with the rabbi at his synagogue for me to come and deliver an eco-justice message. God's promise to Abraham, in saying, "In you all the families of the earth shall be blessed" (Genesis 12:3), took on a new meaning. Since then, whenever anybody asks me to bless the food or give a benediction, I remember the time Ernest blessed me.

Benediction people are desperately needed today—leaders who can offer words of wisdom as a blessing to guide us through times when industrial civilization's foundations shake. Returning from doing research in South America, Alexander Humboldt met with Thomas Jefferson. He told the American president how necessary it was to stop taking land from Indigenous peoples and forcing slaves to cut down forests, replacing balanced ecosystems with European-style plantations, and he warned that if Jefferson did not abolish slavery and end the practice of taking native lands, terrible crises would someday engulf Euro-American civilization. Jefferson, however, did not listen to Humboldt. Instead, he gave his blessing and guidance to what has turned out to be over two centuries of "progress and development."[2]

In July 2022 I was again asked to offer a blessing in Wisconsin. Steve Apfelbaum invited my brother John and me to the dinner where he was to announce the start of a new venture in ecosystem regeneration, Applied Ecological Institute. As we became acquainted with folks at the pre-dinner reception, enjoying the crackers made from perennial ryegrass seed with Wisconsin cheese, in the back of my mind, I thought I might be asked to speak—to do so, I needed an outline and a sense of who I might be addressing. Soon we were at the dinner table, and a soil expert and I began an illuminating conversation. Then Steve stood and asked John Mackey, founder of Whole Foods, to get us started, adding, "After John, I'd like you to say a few words, Owen."

"Once again I'm asked to give a blessing before a meal," I thought to myself, "Steve trusts me a lot to ask me to speak at this organizing meeting, and I really want to bless this effort to regenerate ecosystems. "Help me, Lord," I prayed. In my mind was a rough outline with three points: (1) who I am, (2) eco-justice value signposts, and (3) divine presence that will carry us through. When

John finished, I walked to where I could face everyone, and spoke:

> First, I'm both a Baptist and Methodist minister—I've served churches in both denominations (I felt a surprised, interested response). My parents, during World War II, lived in Cambria, Wisconsin, where we attended the Presbyterian Church. Over the years, I've worshipped in Lutheran, Congregational, and Pentecostal churches, as well as Quaker meetings. I like to fish, and I learned to be a conservationist growing up in Wisconsin, which led me to start the Valley Forge Chapter of Trout Unlimited in Chester County, Pennsylvania. As we struggled to save our local streams, I became friends with nonreligious as well as religious folks who joined in our efforts.
>
> Second, when concerns for ecology and justice come together, value signposts point the way to better days ahead:
>
> - *Reverence for life* occurs when you feel awe and respect for nature, as we did yesterday when Steve, Jason Carlson, and I caught and released native brook trout shining with full spawning colors.
> - *Interdependence with life connects us* as we listen to and work with other people, animals, birds, plants, and soils.
> - *Stewardship of life* begins as we care for the earth and release healing energies.
> - *Integrity in life* happens to us when guided by the values of reverence, interdependence, and stewardship; each day we become healthier and a little more whole.
>
> Third, regenerating nature is grounded in universal loving power, as Psalm 36 tells us. "For with you is the fountain of life; in your light we see light" (verses 8-9). God made

> you and me and gave us these big heads on our shoulders, hands that dig and make, feet that carry us where we decide to go. We are here for a purpose. We will be tempted to advance at others' expense what we see as true. We will face determined opposition. The Light of the World shines—today we take a step on the journey to heal, help, and regenerate nature and people.

Steve Apfelbaum offered his vision for Applied Ecological Institute after we enjoyed a dinner of fresh organic vegetables and grass-fed beef from local farms.

> I have personally started and funded Applied Ecological Institute as a 501(c)(3) nonprofit. Others who have joined in this effort have started providing seed funding for the new companies. What I'm looking for now are investors or philanthropists who want to get involved in these types of new efforts. Thoughts on how to rapidly build support and engage with others who care about the earth and our fellow inhabitants on this wonderful planet would be most appreciated.
>
> At this time, we have the team in place that is focused on scaling rapid climate mitigation solutions grounded in ecosystem restoration. And to catalyze this even faster, we are focused on creating new businesses that come at the ecosystem restoration from completely different angles. The Climate Foods Company has been started with the recently retired twenty-three-year former chairman of Whole Foods. The second company provides a very innovative way to map, value (appraise), and monetize up to 150 to 200 natural resources rights and ecosystem assets found on land. This company (StratyfX) is resulting in

> some really amazing changes. For example, one Eskimo community in Alaska had their land valued for $0.83 per acre. When we mapped, valued, and appraised their land, we certified a value of $4,200 per acre. The new valuation became the value of the communities' assets. Immediately, they had an improvement in asset value of $40 million because they own 90,000 acres in fee. If they choose to move forward, their community could afford to purchase plane tickets to send several members with leukemia to Fairbanks and Anchorage for medical treatments.[3]

At evening's end, many gathered outside. Surrounded by the native prairie that replaced the old golf course greens, as twilight turned to dusk and we relaxed, Steve came over and said, "Owen, you spoke to their hearts tonight."

"Steve," I responded, "my words were a benediction for your efforts to restore the earth. The Hebrew word for heart *(lev)* means the decisional, willing center of a person. I called each to decide to move forward with you in regenerating the ecosystems of this planet."

Living in the Benediction: Turn to Me and Live

We enter the way of life when we turn to God. Blessed by good health, I have lived a long life. Recently, a sense of discomfort after meals led me to a visit with Nurse Chun Du at Kendal's patient care, who scheduled a CT scan that very afternoon. Early the next morning, she called me—there was a mass inside the head of my pancreas that might be malignant. That night I prayed, "Let go and let God." In the morning, I decided to leave what would happen to me in God's hands. "If my time is at an end, that's okay. If you want me to stay longer, that's okay too."

On Monday, July 3, Dr. Lieberman, my general practitioner, broke into his July Fourth holiday to meet with my daughter, Beth, and me to discuss the findings from the CT scan. Without treatment, people with pancreatic cancer live three to six months. "With treatment, Owen, you might live for years, or if the cancer is advanced, you could die soon." He spent over half an hour with us as we struggled with his words' emotional impact.

As a strong man, when I got sick, I sought help, did what the doctor told me to do, and got better. When I had sciatica, for instance, with pain shooting up and down my left leg, I went to physical therapists, did the prescribed exercises, and kept doing them when nothing seemed to happen. Even though healing slows in older folks, I began to feel better and eventually could walk without pain.

When the nurse weighed me, I discovered I had lost eight pounds over the last few months because my body was burning my body fat. So I started eating three big meals a day, ignoring the sense of discomfort and tiredness after each meal. "That surely will result in a weight gain," I thought to myself. After two weeks, I weighed myself again. The scale showed I was barely even. I realized what was happening with my pancreas was beyond my control—my time on earth could soon be over!

Then Joe, my son-in-law, called me. A few weeks before, his mother had died unexpectedly. Fortunately, she had her affairs in order, but he still ended up with weighty responsibilities. "Owen," he said, "make arrangements now so you don't burden your family after you die." The words "after you die" rang in my ears. It was hard to accept I was going to die—soon!

For many years, I have practiced letting go and letting God, praying, "Lord, give me the serenity to accept the things I cannot change, the courage to change the things I can, and the wisdom to know the difference." I woke at 3:00 that morning thinking, "It's me dying." Then the gospel message came home to me: the Lord holds the whole world—and me—in kind, powerful hands. "Lord, I release control of my life and death to you," I prayed. "Help me to do it!" Finally, I fell asleep.

I awoke feeling worry-free, filled with purposeful energy. A call to my lawyer ensured that powers of attorney for my health care and finances were prepared for my daughter. I talked with my credit union about protecting my checking and savings accounts from identity theft. Yet I still had time to go to the store and get a prescription filled for new glasses, and while there, buy protein supplements—drinking a bottle as I drove home. Then I took my wife, Irene, for an afternoon ride to Bailey's dairy farm, enjoying her smiles as she watched a child feeding goats and three ducks waddling out to hop in their water-filled washtub.

Before long, the day came when I was on the way to the University of Pennsylvania Hospital, where Dr. Coughlin performed an endoscopy and took tissue samples of my pancreas's growth. The van driver who transported me said that he had delivered our newspaper for years until suddenly he was told the paper was canceling home deliveries and he was out of a job. "I'm working part-time," he told me, "but driving for Kendal at least covers some of my living expenses." As we entered Interstate 95 on our way into Philadelphia and I saw the city's skyline, I thought, "How out of balance with life is this metropolitan area. How much injustice there is, as with my driver who faithfully delivered papers for so many years." Then we drove past the Philadelphia International Airport, built upon what were fertile wetlands supporting vast flocks of nesting ducks and shorebirds. Now I was riding through an ecological wasteland, with only remnants of life-giving nature, headed toward a powerful, wealthy city that was utterly dependent on food and water outside itself. The multilane highway on which I was riding extended from Portland, Maine, to Miami, Florida, with its cars and trucks burning fossil fuels—and my transportation was adding its little bit of pollution, causing climate change.

Beth met me, and we sat in the waiting room until the orderly took me by wheelchair to the operating room. The doctor explained to us that she would insert the endoscope down into my stomach and into the small intestine, where it rested against the pancreas, take ultrasound pictures, and then insert a tiny needle into the suspicious mass and take cells for a pathology report. As often happens, procedures took longer than expected. A nurse tucked warm blankets around me so I would be comfortable, and another inserted the hollow needle in a vein to administer anesthetic.

Suddenly Dr. Coughlin stood beside my gurney, asking about concerns I might have. "Please minimize the amount of anesthetic," I requested, "but I'm not worried about what you'll discover. I've turned control of what will happen over to the Lord. If I'm to die soon, that's okay, and if I'm to live longer, that's okay too." Soon I was in the operating room, attended by a team of several nurses and the anesthesiologist. A warm, foggy feeling came over me, and I was out until I awakened in the recovery room.

"Everything went well," a nurse explained, "no complications."

Soon I rode back home with my daughter. Feeling a bit worn but not nauseated or dizzy, I walked without difficulty from the car into my cottage, where Kendal at Longwood's food service had a liquid meal waiting for me. After I ate, I still felt hungry. "I wish I had solid food," I said to Beth. She went up to Kendal's dining room and brought back some lasagna. It tasted good. Staying with me until she was sure I was okay, Beth hugged me and was on her way.

A few days later, the pathologist's report arrived, which Nurse Chun Du reviewed with Beth and me. The irregular mass in the head of the pancreas was indeed malignant. That evening, around 6:00, surely after a long workday, Dr. Coughlin called and asked, "Have you seen the report?"

"Yes, I have, but I'll have to wait for the appointment with the oncologist to understand it," I responded. "Dr. Coughlin," I continued, "you did an outstanding procedure. My throat wasn't scratched, and I was only a little hoarse the next day." As she thanked me and concluded the conversation, I felt caring sadness in her voice, leaving me with a premonition that when the oncologist interpreted her findings, the news would be dire.

Blessings flowed into my life when I accepted my death. Every time I turned over to the Lord my whole self, the next day I was not only free to be myself, filled with purposeful energy, but also happy—even joyful. Whenever I remembered Dr. Lieberman's saying that, without treatment, people with pancreatic cancer lived only three to six months, I laughed out loud! "I may die soon," I said to myself. "Why am I laughing?" Immediately, I remembered I decided last fall to give myself the kind of care I had given to Irene, beginning physical therapy to heal sciatic injuries and going to an integrative health doctor to revitalize my digestive system. "Over the past months, I've done daily exercises, walked a mile a day, and changed my whole diet," I reflected. "Now my back and leg are almost back to normal, and my digestive system is working well, but in a few weeks, I'm going to die and my body will return to the soil from which it came! That's so unexpected, it's funny!" Then I realized my life would end soon.

Starting with my separation and divorce from my first wife, Sharon, my goal has been to heal my family tree. I set this goal following a 1987 assignment by Dr. McAll, priest and psychotherapist, to go to Communion and invite family members to go with me, for Jesus Christ is especially present in the broken bread and shared wine at the Lord's Supper. Attending the Lord's Supper alone for many years, I asked the Lord to forgive my faults and failures, and I forgave those in the family who hurt me. Year after year, nothing seemed to change. Then I sensed it was time to get in touch with Martin, my youngest son. At my invitation, he came over to my home. We forgave each other and embraced with a big hug. His new wife, Tonya, became a loving member of the Owens family.

Over the next few years, Beth stayed in touch with me, but my son Andrew was distant. Last year I heard Andrew had a new partner, Julie, and I invited them to go with me to The Mountaintop, a play about the last night of Dr. Martin Luther King's life. Not only did they go with me, but they also took me out to dinner before the play and paid the bill! I felt cared for as Andrew drove us to the play and parked and as we entered the theater and sat down.

When the angel the Lord assigned to prepare Dr. King for his death appeared in his room as an attractive woman carrying the coffee he ordered, the two actors' dialogue revealed the civil rights martyr as a real man. Deeply moved, I cried frequently. As we walked to their car, Julie said, "I cried a lot and so did Andrew." Right then, I knew we had taken a big step to heal our family tree.

When Beth volunteered to come to the unexpected appointment with Dr. Lieberman on July 3, interrupting her own family holiday, again, I felt especially loved, as I did when she spent the day with me during the diagnostic procedure and drove me home.

Finally, the day arrived when we would get a diagnosis and possible treatment for my malignancy. Once again I felt loved when Andrew, Martin, and Beth went with me for the diagnostic appointment with Dr. Quinn, the oncologist. With anticipation, we entered Dr. Quinn's office, meeting a young physician with impressive credentials. He showed us pictures of my cancer, the lesions inside the pancreas and on my gall bladder, and probable lymph node metastases. Clearly and honestly, Dr. Quinn said, "Owen, the cancer has metastasized. We might try chemotherapy to slow it down, but its effects would be limited, and the treatment would make you sick. Your quality of life would drop, and you would suffer and maybe die even sooner than without treatment. I can't tell you how long you have to live, but it may be a few weeks or months." He concluded by offering to get a second opinion if we wanted one. Going around our family circle, I asked each if he or she had questions, to which the doctor responded.

Knowing your dad is going to die stirs deep sadness—a sadness that can trigger the denial of painful truth. Instead, each chose to face and accept a painful diagnosis. I was proud of my children's strength, even more so when we went back to my home, and I led them in talking about what they heard and ways we might respond to what the doctor said. "Dad, you are strong," Beth said. "You look like you're seventy years old. You may live a lot longer than a few weeks or months." Martin and Andrew felt the same. Martin shared his experience with his late wife, Tonya's, cancer, and strongly felt that, as the doctor suggested, we should not do useless treatments that would leave me sick and weak. Andrew concurred, then added, "But I wonder if a second opinion might be a good idea." When each left, I got one hug after another, leaving me with a prayer assignment to accept the prognosis and once again turn my life and death over to the Lord.

After dinner I called to tell my brother what happened. Picking up the phone was hard. John and I have been through so much together—when something happened to me, my brother always helped in any way he could. Single, living alone for many years, who would look after him when he needed loving care at the end of his life if I died? Worries slipped away when he answered the phone. As I shared the diagnosis, we were together as we considered what the doctor said.

Before bed that night, I let go and let God. Early the next morning, I didn't wake up thinking about dying. Instead, I was filled with joy on that new day. "What a happy month July has been, Lord," I prayed. "If this cancer sparked all this loving care, from both my family and friends, how can I complain? This has been the most joy-filled month in my life. You have blessed me beyond measure. However long I live, let each of my days resonate with your glory."

Then I thanked the Lord Jesus Christ for the love that poured over me. At the same time, I reflected on the Gospel of John's sayings that Jesus was the only way to God the Father and thought about all my other religious and nonreligious friends who experienced the same love I did. I knew God forgave everyone who turned to the Lord, in whatever way they understood God. So I continued to pray that the same forgiving, covenant-keeping love would reach out to all and flow through the world.

Experiencing the joy when I turned control over my death and life to the Lord, I remembered what Maurice Friedman said about dialogue and trust:

> In order to persevere in the Hasidic way of life, one does not need a special grace or faith in a set creed. But one does need trust—existential trust, trust in God, trust that God addresses us in the happenings of everyday life, and that we can make our lives real by responding to that address. For the Hasidim, as for biblical man, God's hiding was as real as his revealing himself, and when God hid himself, it was difficult to maintain one's trust.[4]

My mentor James Muilenberg, professor of the Hebrew Scriptures, said that knowing the Lord was as intimate and personal as when in Genesis 4:1, Adam *knew* his wife, Eve, and she conceived and bore Cain. While the Hebrew verb for "to know" caught up the sexual intimacy of wife and husband, it also meant to discern, discriminate, acknowledge, and possess. Muilenberg reminded us, therefore, that for the Hebrews, the "flaw" in human beings was not in our intellect (nor physical bodies), but in our will. "It was not a matter of being unable to think clearly but of living in accordance with the divine will and purpose."[5]

Communication between and among beings happens in dialogue when we listen to and speak with each other. The One who addresses us in the exact circumstances of our lives is the living, speaking Lord, who proves to be steadfastly loving, making and keeping promises, assuring that when we live by faith, we will live "to the max" now and forever (see Psalm 36 and 37; Romans 5:1-5). When we trust in the Lord, wait for daily guidance, and take another step on the way of life, we make our lives real.

God's hiding, however, is as real as the Holy Spirit's presence. Deep communion may be followed by a time when the all-beneficent One seems absent. After fifteen hundred years of Christian discrimination, persecution, murderous pogroms, and the Holocaust, Jews know how difficult it has been to maintain trust in God, who is good and powerful, as human-caused suffering destroys the lives of wonderful people and threatens us with loss and death: "The favorite disciple of Rabbi Pinhas complained to him that it was very difficult in adversity to retain perfect faith in the belief that God provides for every human being. 'It actually seems as if God were hiding his face from such an unhappy being,' he exclaimed. 'It ceases to be a hiding,' replied Rabbi Pinhas, 'if you know it is a hiding.'"[6]

Though the Spirit of God used my cancer to surround me with caring love, the words of Rabbi Pinhas's disciple remind me that dark nights of the soul may be coming. The Lord seemed to be saying, *Don't forget, Owen, that there are times when it's necessary for me to hide myself. Remember what Rabbi Pinhas taught: "It ceases to be a hiding if you know it's a hiding." When you feel like you are walking alone through the valley of the shadow of death, lift up pain and suffering to me and trust in me. No matter what happens, you'll be okay—I am the living God.*

Conclusion

When we turn to the Lord, we live and become benediction people like our Creator. When we let go and let God, floods of love and light pour into our lives. Hard times that come upon us call us to renew decisions we made to trust in the Lord and wait patiently for the Spirit again to come close and shine kindly light.

Notes

1. Margaret Barker, *Creation* (T&T Clark, 2010), 250–73.

2. Alexander Humboldt pioneered an understanding of nature using both rigorous scientific and poetic feeling. In 1800 he observed that Lake Valencia in Columbia was rapidly drying up due to European planters using slave labor, which he detested, to deforest arable land and the mountains: "The sward and moss disappearing with the brushwood from the sides of the mountains, the waters falling in rain are no longer impeded in their course, and instead of slowly augmenting the level of the rivers by progressive filtration, they furrow during heavy showers the sides of the hills, bear down the loosened soil, and form those sudden inundations that devastate the country." Humboldt's insights shaped the work of Darwin, Thoreau, Marsh, Muir, and a host of less famous people. Land and water conservation movements in America, in which I have played a small part, were generated by honest, scientific, brilliant people like Humboldt. Andrea Wulf, *The Invention of Nature* (Vintage Books, 2015), 65, and see chapters 17–23.

3. Steven Apfelbaum, a speech given in July 2022 for a benefit for the Applied Ecological Institute.

4. Maurice Friedman, *A Dialogue with Hasidic Tales: Hallowing the Everyday* (Insight, 1988), 123.

5. James Muilenberg, *The Way of Israel: Biblical Faith and Ethics* (Harper & Row: Torchbooks, 1965), 17.

6. Maurice Friedman, *A Dialogue with Hasidic Tales: Hallowing the Everyday* (Human Sciences Press, 1988), 123.

CHAPTER 7

Love Lights the Way

Everybody wants to be loved and to love. Yet we live in a world in which love seems impossible. As my wife, Irene, and I experienced her memory slipping away, Psalm 36 shone with the Lord's steadfast covenant love, resounding with a message of hope. Love lights the way.

Psalm 36 Takes Us to the Loving One Who Made Us

Imagine this: Planet Earth is held together by unbounded love—steady, faithful, absolutely dependable.

> Your steadfast love, O Lord, extends to the heavens,
> your faithfulness to the clouds.
> Your righteousness is like the mighty mountains;
> your judgments are like the great deep;
> you save humans and animals alike, O Lord.
> —Psalm 36:5-6

The New Interpreter's Bible states that Psalm 36 teaches that "God's character is built into the very structure of the universe. Everything and every creature—'humans and animals alike'—depends on God for its existence and future."[1] A righteous God is able and willing to set the planet and all life upon it right again. Like the inexhaustible power of surging oceans are the Lord's just judgments, saving humans and animals alike.

Margaret Barker unpacks the key words of Psalm 36:

> Justice and righteousness, loving kindness, faithfulness, and peace describe the atonement and covenant process. . . . The first step is justice, *mispat*, better translated judgment, recognizing what needs to be done to uphold the covenant. A judgment is a wise decision, and so when Solomon decided to give the baby to its natural mother: 'All Israel heard the *judgment* . . . they perceived that the wisdom of God was in him to render justice (one Hebrew word, *mispat*, is here translated by two English words, justice and judgment).[2]

No matter what threats and dangers, in the Lord's temple of nature, *all* people can find safe refuge in the shadow of their Creator's wings. There, people have more than enough to eat. Clear, pure, delightfully tasting water satisfies every thirst. "For with you is the fountain of life; in your light we see light" (verses 8-9).

Those who worship in the temple, pictured in Psalm 36, however, are painfully aware of the suffering that human evildoing causes. "Transgression speaks to the wicked deep in their hearts; there is no fear of God before their eyes" (verse 1). The wicked put themselves in the place of God. They cease to act wisely and do good. They even plot evil as they lie in bed, thinking of ways to get ahead by doing in somebody else. "I'll get mine by taking away yours!" they say. "I'm smart, tough, powerful—you'd better follow me and do what I say, or else!" Centering their lives on themselves, they set out on a way that is not good and do not reject evil (verses 1-4). Seeking complete control, perceiving no reason to be accountable to the One who is truth and love, sinners choose the wrong way and miss the mark. They have no stability, therefore, no rootedness, no place to stand.[3]

The Most High's love makes us whole again. Facing our own faults and compassion for others come together when we worship the Lord, outdoors or indoors. The *Jewish Study Bible* says that Psalm 36 is about the temple in Jerusalem, where the righteous sought God. "Though He is worshipped in the temple, God's beneficent justice is of cosmic proportions, reaching everywhere."[4] When a Jew puts on a prayer shawl, tallit, prayer begins by reciting the three verses from Psalm 36 that begin and end with God's steadfast love (verses 6-8, Tanakh).

The Hebrew word *hesed* (translated as kindness, mercy, and steadfast love) describes the everlasting covenant established on day one of Creation (Genesis 1). When human beings are saved by the Lord's *hesed*, we practice loving and become, as the Hebrew puts it, *hasiyd*, as in the Hasidic movement in Judaism. Truth and love are inseparable. Since God is kind and just, those who follow the Spirit's leading do justice, love kindness, and walk humbly with God (Micah 6:8). Barker writes, "The result of kindness and good judgment is righteousness (*sdqh*), which means both the state when the covenant was restored and also the actions that made this happen."[5] A righteous person, therefore, is actively related to God, to other persons, and to the wider creation, following the Lord in healing broken relationships, faithfully seeking to hold together the bonds that make it possible to live on planet Earth.

Living Fully

When we taste, touch, see, hear, and feel everything like a child, we are happy and feel good, and are fully alive. Thinking about times when I felt fully alive, I remember an Owens family picnic at the Madison, Wisconsin, zoo. My dad took us to see Annie the elephant. My brother and I held peanuts out to her in our little hands, and her trunk's tiny bristles brushed my hand as she grasped the peanut and put it in her mouth. Then it was time for the picnic lunch. How good those deviled eggs were—and the coleslaw and chopped ham sandwiches. I can taste them right now.

Getting in tune with God's love enables us to live life "to the max." In spring 2018, my son Martin invited me to stay a few days at his house to attend a men's retreat at his church. The pastors, John and Isha Edmondson, who birthed Victory in Christ Christian Center in Westville, New Jersey, wanted to show God's people how to make Jesus Christ their Savior and also Lord over every area of their lives. A thriving multicultural church, Victory has a twenty-first-century vision of reaching the lost, maturing believers, and raising up godly leaders to be equipped for their purpose and calling.

Shortly after I arrived, our daughter-in-law Tonya shared disturbing news, "Dad Owen, not long ago, when I saw a spider hanging down right over our bed, I jumped out so fast I fell on the floor. My side really hurt, and a few days later, a lump appeared. When we checked it out, I was diagnosed with stage three and a half breast cancer. I'm not telling people I have cancer," Tonya continued, "except for a few who will not feel sorry for me but will be with me in what's going to be a victorious battle—I know the Lord will heal me."

I felt honored by Tonya's trust but was deeply concerned and also wondered about her secrecy—she had not told even her pastors nor members of her immediate family. As the retreat moved forward, Martin and I prayed for the Spirit to heal her. On Saturday afternoon, women were invited to join the men in a service led by prophets selected by the pastors because of their inspirational and healing gifts. Beginning with congregational singing, prayer, and biblical messages, Prophet David Perrin moved into the congregation and, as he was led, went to individuals in the congregation, held his hands over them, and prayed for them. Martin was standing next to an aisle, Tonya next to him, and I was on her left. Prophet Perrin came to us, and as he prayed, I saw Martin sway as though he would fall and then steady himself as Tonya started to drop to the floor. Martin held on to her and guided her body back into her chair.

Never had I seen anyone in our family "slain in the Spirit" before, but I had no time to reflect as the service progressed. When men were invited forward for guiding prayer, recognizing I needed all the help I could get, I got up and stood with the row of men. When Prophet David came to me, he placed his hands on my head, prayed, and then quietly whispered, "You have much life in you, and you will finish strong!"

Living life fully took on new meaning after the service. Confident in God's healing power, Tonya did whatever was necessary to get well, no matter how much pain and suffering she had. After a radical mastectomy, radiation, and reconstructive surgery, her health returned in 2018. To celebrate recovery and witness to God's love in Christ that makes us more than conquerors, she and Martin planned a dinner at a prominent facility that she had used before. Most were friends from Victory in Christ Christian Center, but many from our family were included. Martin, with his resonating, melodious voice, showed TV news clips of Tonya speaking at the Philadelphia march of survivors of breast cancer.

The dinner was ample, well-served, and tasty. I was enjoying conversations with people at my table when a tall, tired-looking man made his way into the hall. Tonya saw him and took the mike, "Why, it's Doctor Newman, who did my cancer surgery. You've just finished a long day of surgery. We are honored to have you here and are so glad to see you!"

One of Tonya's assistants showed the doctor to a seat at a prominent table. Though everyone else had almost finished dinner, in a few minutes, the hotel manager brought the doctor a fresh, hot dinner. "How like Tonya," I thought. "She is aware of everything going on, managing an event so that everyone feels welcome, particularly recognizing and honoring this special latecomer."

Love Lights the Way

As Tonya fought cancer, Irene and I struggled to understand and deal with my wife's increasing loss of memory and the paranoid fears that went with it. Paranoid dementia is a disease that devastates not only those who suffer from it but also those who care for them. In the middle of a pleasant morning, for instance, I would hear a plaintive question: "Where are my car keys? Did you take them?"

If I pulled back from whatever I was doing and said, "No, I did not," immediately the question would be repeated with more emotional force, "Yes, you did—you were the only one here; tell me what you did with them."

I needed help. In my morning prayer and meditation time, I read Psalm 36 each day, feeling lifted by its message that the earth and all of us on it are held in God's everlasting arms. When memory loss and protective anger were occasional, I could keep my calm, but when they became more constant, I felt I was walking on eggshells. When I found myself arguing that I had nothing to do with losing something, an angry exchange would happen. It was even harder to respond to the sad complaint, "You don't talk with me!"

"Am I at fault?" I wondered. "Should I listen and talk more?" Most troubling of all, however, were the words, "You don't love me!" Though I was with my wife most of the time, providing constant care and support, there was always more I could be doing.

Often, reasoning with Irene had distressing consequences. I might say, "You were worried about people stealing your purse. Let's stop and think about the last time you had it." Less and less able to remember, she would try to get control by repeating, "Don't deny. You took it!" Sometimes she might have an all-day emotional reaction with tears and angry outbursts.

As the disease progressed, I felt more emotionally and physically exhausted. Then a daily reading from *One Day at a Time in Al-Anon* started me thinking, namely, that a wide gap existed between what

I believed about being justified by God's loving grace and how it applied to my daily living: "In Al-Anon I discover two roadblocks that have kept me from seeing the value and comfort of the spiritual approach: *self-justification and self-righteousness*. The first gives a grim certainty that I'm always right; the second smothers me in the delusion that I'm better than other people—'holier than thou.'"[6]

The next time I heard, "You took my purse," I was about to say, "I did no such thing." Then I realized, "I'm trying to justify myself because I'm right and she's wrong!" Later I journaled about what happened, and when I could let go and let God and not justify myself, the result was calming for both of us.

A song I heard began to resonate within me, and as I replayed the oratorio *Elijah* again and again, the words came alive:

> Oh rest in the Lord, wait patiently for him,
> And he shall give thee thy heart's desire.
>
> Commit thy way unto him, and trust in him;
> And fret not thyself because of evildoers,
>
> O rest in the Lord, wait patiently for him.
> Wait patiently for him.

The song was written by Mendelssohn, and I discovered the words came from Psalm 37, which says, "Trust in the LORD and do good; live in the land and enjoy security" (verse 3). On the preceding page of the Bible was Psalm 36 about the Lord's steadfast covenant love. When the next angry accusation flew at me, I found myself silently singing, "Oh rest in the Lord," and felt quieted. As I waited before responding, a loving response came to mind. "Ah, so that is what the twelve-step program means about detaching in love," I mused.

As Irene's paranoia worsened and she angrily asserted that I had taken something, I sang silently for a moment. Resting in the Lord freed me for a crucial moment—not to react in self-defense, but to respond with loving detachment. Looking back on such silent moments, all my skills, all I learned, all that I am came together in a quiet, decisive moment to rest in the Lord—and I did let go and let God. When I gave up trying to control my wife, what I've wanted all my life—to be loved and to love—happened.

Freedom from long-buried trauma comes when we allow love's light to shine into our inner darkness. Deep feelings from the times we were exploited and abused as children sooner or later surface, breaking into view like the tip of an immense iceberg. Driving the self-protecting weapon of flaming anger is not only anxiety and fear, but also, on the deepest level, intense shame and guilt.

As Irene's memory lapses and paranoid episodes worsened, she and I had many helpful sessions with Kendal's social worker and therapist, Vicki Center. In earlier sessions, Irene and I talked with Vicki about a possible move so my wife could get more help. Vicki prepared the necessary consent form for the move, which Irene signed.

Irene's daughter Amy and I scheduled a session with Vicki. This session was particularly important because I could no longer provide the kind of supportive care Irene needed—soon she would require the kind of nursing provided in Kendal's part- or full-care facility. Perhaps sensing what was going to happen, when it was time for the session with Vicki, Irene said, "I don't want to go. You go!"

"This time with Vicki is for both of us," I replied. "Come up by yourself—I'll meet you there."

Amy met me at Vicki's office, and then Irene did show up, and we entered together. Vicki started by asking each of us to give our concerns. As the conversation progressed, I could feel Irene's tension building.

Imagine what it's like when you've always kept the family's financial books and numbers no longer make sense to you. Imagine what it's like when you go for a walk and realize you don't know the way home. Imagine you've always kept your home in order, and now you forget how to turn the stove on and off. Imagine what it's like when you have always taken care of yourself and now need somebody with you to guide and help. Imagine becoming incontinent when you have always kept yourself and your clothes clean. Imagine being afraid of somebody stealing from you, hiding your purse, and then you can't find it, not remembering you hid it. Imagine trying to get some control by blaming somebody else for taking your purse.

In twelve-step programs, people share about the elephant in the room that nobody talks about even though it's there. Amy and I both had experienced times when Irene angrily blamed us for something, but these happened only in the family, never out in public. Then suddenly, even though the therapist was right there, Irene angrily pointed her finger at me and said, "I told you I didn't want to come here today, and you made me do it!"

Hurt people hurt people. Light shining in darkness reveals underneath self-protective anger a little girl or boy who has been shamed again and again by a parent or sibling and is close to drowning in their own pool of tears.

When a blaming finger is pointed at a husband and that finger shakes with intense anger, even a skilled therapist shielded by learnings from decades of counseling feels a palpitating heart. Surging, blaming anger can slip through the strongest protective shields. I surely felt it and sang silently, "O rest in the Lord," with no idea how to respond. Fortunately, our counselor seemed to shine with a warm, kind light. Fearful anger dissolved as she calmly said, "Irene, I feel how upset you are. I'm here to help, and so are Owen and Amy." By the end of the session, Irene agreed that it was time for her to move to where she could get full-time assistance.

On day one of Creation, divine love brought into being all that is—and it was good. If and when hard-earned healing skills allow deeply submerged hurts to surface, generational trauma endlessly repeated suddenly is interrupted by a despairing, angry, tearful cry for help. Hearing that cry, Someone with infinite mercy shines with a halo of accepting, freeing love: Don't be ashamed. I made you, your body, desires, mind, and feelings. You are created good, and all the hurt and pain others have put on you, and how in response you have feared and cut down others—all that is bringing you to me like a hurt child running to his mother, who finds himself surrounded in a warm, strong embrace. I am merciful, and I have mercy on all my children. I love you. You are safe now!

Sometimes those who are giving care must reach out for help. At Kendal Crosslands Communities, as we need increasing assistance, we move from independent living cottages into our part- or full-care facility. In January 2019 Irene had a ministroke and returned from the hospital to a room in Cumberland, our limited-care facility, but was unhappy there and wanted desperately to go home. Kendal pioneered in untying the elderly—elders who wander and get lost have a band on an ankle that locks exit doors, but somehow Irene got out and soon was hopelessly lost. A kindly driver picked her up along a dangerous road some distance away. Fortunately, she remembered the address of our cottage. I was waiting when he dropped her off, but her getting lost was only the beginning of a harrowing afternoon.

Refusing to return to assisted living, Irene tried to put everything in the living room and bedroom back in order. Not remembering when we gave my mother's china cabinet to Martin and Tonya for their new home, she questioned, "Where's my china cabinet? It's gone! Did you take it?" Nothing I said was calming. Two nurses came to help her get back to Cumberland. "No! You're trying to take me out of my own home. I'm calling the police!"

This was the second time Irene called 911 for help, and the police officer who came was experienced in helping people who had dementia. "I can't take you in the police car, but the nurses will get a car. I'm going to Cumberland. Will you meet me there?" Irene agreed, got in the van with the nurses, and accepted the officer's authority to settle down in her room.

Though Irene did not escape again, her paranoia worsened. Nurses and other residents did all they could to make her feel welcome and comfortable. Sometimes she smiled a lot, assisted others, and enjoyed the activities. Other times she was upset and angry. One cool March morning in 2019, our nursing director and social worker asked me to meet with them.

"Owen, Irene is so confused and angry, it's almost impossible to care for her. The other day, she even called the police! We need help. Chestnut Hill Hospital can examine Irene and adjust her medications. Will you agree to take her there tonight?"

"Yes, I'll take her there," I replied.

In no way was I going to drive at night to Chestnut Hill. As soon as the meeting ended, I called Martin and asked for help. "Sure," he responded, "I'll ask Tonya—she's good with this."

"Dad Owen, what time should I get there?" Tonya asked.

"Come later in the afternoon when they'll have the papers for admission and have Irene ready."

Tonya and I had dinner together at our café, and then we took Irene in a wheelchair to Tonya's car. My wife and I sat in the back seat together for the hour-long drive to the psychiatric hospital. Irene was fascinated by the big outdoor dinner Tonya was planning for her family the next summer, had suggestions about arrangements, and even volunteered to help. We arrived after 8:00 p.m., but the person at the desk was waiting for us and started the admissions process. By the time we finished, it was late. I was proud of Irene, who drew on tough-minded strengths to complete the entry tests and protocols.

Tonya stayed with us throughout the evening, helping whenever she could. We took the elevator to the psychiatric care floor. The nurse in charge took us to Irene's room, leading us through a locked ward. Moans and cries of troubled persons echoed in the hall even at that late hour. We hugged, said goodbye, and left her there. The next few days were not going to be easy for a once-strong, independent-minded person.

We left at 1:30 in the morning. Roads were almost deserted. Martin called us, followed on his cell phone the route we were taking, gave driving suggestions, and stayed on the phone until we arrived home. Tonya slept what was left of the night at our cottage. In the morning, I fixed breakfast. Then we talked about what I learned from seeking structural change of institutions toward ecological wholeness and social justice at their points of intersection. I wanted to learn more about her African American great-grandmother, who earned enough to buy land in Woodbury, New Jersey, and built houses with her own hands. Conversation about biblical insights into life's meaning and many other matters also flowed until, all too soon, she had to leave. When I thanked her for all she had done, Tonya replied, "Now, Dad Owen, that's what family does!"

Strangely enough, suffering may cause special times when we live life "to the max." Tonya's time of remission from cancer was all too short, as it reappeared in her lungs in 2019. Wanting to live, she fought the disease with courage and constant prayer, enduring painful suffering from surgery, radiation, and chemotherapy, only to discover the cancer had metastasized in her brain. Once again she faced what had happened and underwent radical brain surgery to get well. Her ability to speak and remember began to slip away. She went back to the hospital for treatment, but after tests and scans, the doctors felt they had done all they could. As Tonya went deeper in prayer, she heard the Lord saying that the Spirit would soon carry her home.

My son Martin told me Tonya was getting weaker every day, and I knew I must visit. A year before, Tonya shifted to an organic diet, so I had planted her favorite vegetables in my garden. Tomatoes, fresh sweet corn, frozen spinach, zucchini, cucumbers—I took enough for an army! When I arrived, Tonya was in a bed in the family room next to the kitchen. It was so good to see her again.

"How shall I fix the sweet corn?" Martin asked.

"Boil it in the pan I use," Tonya responded.

Soon the aroma of sweet corn was in the air. Tonya asked to sit on the edge of the bed, facing the couch where I was sitting, and proceeded to eat not one but two ears of corn! Then we had lettuce, tomato, and vegetarian bacon sandwiches. Tonya seemed to delight in each bite. Gardening is fine exercise, and giving produce to those who need food is satisfying, but when someone I know and love ate what I raised, I felt so good.

When we finished eating, we prayed together. Martin and a friend who was there helped Tonya lie back down, and then, after a while, assisted her to change positions to alleviate intense pain. Before I left, Tonya smiled and said, "I love you, Dad Owen."

A few days after I visited Tonya and Martin's home, they participated in a Zoom talk with Irene and me. Tonya had practiced being a loving woman for many years. Learning to love and receive love carried her to the end. Though she had taught women in her church that they were beautiful and how to look that way, particularly important when so many still judge African American people by the color of their skin, the cancer and radiation treatments left Tonya bald, her physical beauty gone. No longer able to sit up, she was lying on her side. Speaking took great effort. Yet her brown eyes shone with light as she said, "Mom Irene, I love you."

Irene replied with warmth, "Tonya, I love you too."

Those words to Irene were the last words of Tonya I heard. Within a few days, she died.

Those who love God and their neighbors as themselves, as did Tonya Owens, show us that suffering and death are not the end. Throughout her life, she excelled in crossing racial and class barriers, bringing people together in loving ways. Tonya's life witnessed that when we love, we are more than conquerors.

Conclusion

God's steadfast love never denies our losses and suffering. The Spirit teaches us to face whatever happens and enlighten our minds. Those who seek refuge under the shadow of the everlasting arms experience the fountain of life that brought us into being and provides food and water until we die. Loved, we decide to love, pray to love, organize for love, and forgive and love our enemies. Then we see miracles happen every day as the Spirit once again saves humans and animals alike. Love lights the way!

Notes

1. J. Clinton McCann, "The Book of Psalms," *The New Interpreter's Bible* (Abingdon, 1996), 14:822.

2. The God of *mispat* is manifest in the order of nature, where *mispat* means seasons and times of the year and is translated as "ordinances" (Isaiah 30:18, Jeremiah 8:7). Moreover, the entitlement of priests from the people, again Hebrew *mispat*, is translated "due" (Deuteronomy 18:3). *Mispat*'s primary meaning is whatever action is in harmony with the divine order. Margaret Barker, *Creation* (T&T Clark, 2010), 162.

3. McCann, "The Book of Psalms," 14:684.

4. *The Jewish Study Bible–Tanakh Translation*, ed. Adele Berlin and Marc Zvi Brettler (Oxford University Press, Jewish Publication Society, 2004), 1321.

5. Barker, *Creation*, 153.

6. *One Day at a Time in Al-Anon* (Al-Anon Family Group Headquarters, 1975), 112.

CHAPTER 8

Grieve and Praise God

This chapter deals with suffering, death, and grief. When I see a West Virginia baby dying because coal mining has poisoned the air and water, how do I make sense out of what happened? How do I account for our daughter-in-law, Tonya's, death from cancer when she lived so close to the Lord? Unmerited suffering takes us to the biblical story of Job, who lost his children and everything he had.

Sometimes I Feel Like a Motherless Child

Christianity teaches that Jesus loves the children, their mothers and fathers, everybody, and even more—that the Lord holds the whole world in loving hands. Yet weighty objections exist to the testimony that in, with, and under all life is light, warmth, love shining from the face of God. Is it really true that it is loving hands that hold the universe? If so, how do we find such love? How do we reflect God's self-giving love when we ourselves are crushed down and suffering?

I feel these painful questions when loved ones are devastated by memory loss or disease, or personal crises pile up all at once, such as the loss of a home, a job, or a child, spouse, or parent. Painful questions arise when our nation is divided by hatred and when it seems no one is listening or telling the truth—just getting power and control. We also find ourselves asking difficult questions when we hear about families and children driven from their homes by wars, drought, gangs, or human trafficking, and they drag themselves over deserts or raging seas to the borders of other nations only to be turned away, separated from their children, or placed in dangerous refugee camps for years on end. We wonder if the planet and systems of life will survive the pollution and waste we generate and the greed of corporations that oppress.

When we look at nature, we see predation as an elemental fact of life. Planet Earth itself, moreover, not only generates life but also experiences catastrophes large and small, as when an asteroid slammed into it and wiped out dinosaurs and most of the rest of life. Humans create misery as the strong exploit the vulnerable and human-caused climate change unravels planetary systems of life. Religions teach that the Source of life cares for us, but it is hard to believe when we see the suffering and death caused by wars of conquest and persecution of those with different beliefs from theirs. After earthquakes and wars, silence reigns until cries of the survivors echo: "We have lost all! Does anyone care?" We know deep within what it means to love and be loved, yet, "if the foundations are destroyed, what can the righteous do?" (Psalm 11:3).

As an evangelical minister, I owe a great debt to the Puritans and deeply treasure a rich theological and spiritual inheritance.[1] One summer my wife and I sailed from Newport, Rhode Island, to Nantucket. When the Puritans first arrived, whales were reportedly so numerous that one could almost walk on their backs from the shore to Nantucket! Now, right whales are almost extinct, and sighting any whale species is a rare treat.

Puritan New England targeted the whales. They were killed without limit to make whale oil. When the Atlantic whales were almost gone, whaling ships went to the Pacific to continue their profitable slaughter. Within my generation, the same process repeated itself with the cod fishery. Huge factory ships dredged the ocean, targeting the most profitable species. The fishery was destroyed. When my wife and I visited the Stellwagen Banks off Cape Cod, no fishing boats remained on what was still an immensely fertile ocean. Fertile, yes, but also virtually fishless! No fish—no fishing!

"Sometimes I feel like a motherless child," laments the spiritual, expressing how I felt as we sailed off Nantucket across watery voids. As I looked at a sea without whales, I felt betrayed by my religious ancestors. How could Puritans who were inspired by the heavenly vision of establishing the kingdom of God in North America give themselves to kill the whales? How could they exterminate the Pequots and other indigenous Americans? Why did they justify genocidal wars by quoting Scripture, saying that as God's chosen people, they had a right to take the land? How could they allow greed to replace God?

"Sometimes I feel like I'm almost gone," the spiritual continues. When I see the desolation wrought by the creation's unmakers, I am led to Job, a righteous man bowed down with loss and sickness. In Psalms and Deuteronomy, indeed throughout the Bible, Scriptures affirm that the righteous will prosper. Despite afflictions, the man who conducts his affairs with justice will be blessed with wealth and descendants (Psalm 112). Yet Job, a deeply righteous man, lost everything.

Job's suffering came from both human and ecological sources. War and wind brought misery. A messenger came to Job and said,

> "The oxen were plowing and the donkeys were feeding beside them, and the Sabeans fell on them and carried them off and killed the servants with the edge of the sword; I alone have escaped to tell you." . . . While he was still speaking, another came and said, "Your sons and daughters were eating and drinking wine in their eldest brother's house, and suddenly a great wind came across the desert, struck the four corners of the house, and it fell on the young people, and they are dead; I alone have escaped to tell you." (Job 1:14-15,18-19)

Losing animals and servants was bad enough, for they were the engines of prosperity, but worse was the death of Job's children—

with them, Job's future died. Then Job was afflicted with loathsome sores from head to foot! Having lost everything, Job sat upon all that remained of his civilization—a garbage heap! After the crash, all that was left of growth and development was rotting rubble. We children of the twentieth and twenty-first centuries turn to Job not only because he experienced suffering, but also because what came to him was not his fault. He was "blameless and upright, one who feared God and turned away from evil" (Job 1:1).

Modern nations fear an end to unlimited expansion. Remembering the terrible war and the Holocaust triggered by the Great Depression of 1929, leaders tolerate sweatshops and the worldwide destruction of fisheries. The main goal of domestic and foreign policy has been to keep the economy growing. "What is going to happen to us?" biologist Edward O. Wilson wondered. "Are we racing toward the brink of an abyss, or are we just gathering speed for a takeoff to a wonderful future?"[2] He posited two answers to his question: *exemptionalism* or *environmentalism*.

> The first, *exemptionalism*, holds that since humankind is transcendent in intelligence and spirit, our species must have been released from the iron laws of ecology that bind all other species. However serious the problem, civilized human beings, by ingenuity, force of will, and—who knows—divine dispensation, will find a solution. The opposing idea of reality is environmentalism, which sees humanity as a biological species tightly dependent on the natural world. However formidable our intellect may be and however fierce our spirit, the argument goes, those qualities are not enough to free us from the constraints of the natural environment in which the human ancestors evolved."[3]

Human beings working together have great power, celebrated in the obsolete slogan "The sky's the limit!" The slogan is outdated, of course, because astronauts have walked on the moon, making it seem that even the boundaries of space are irrelevant. God spoke to Job, the Bible's master naturalist, in ways that puzzle us: "Can you draw out Leviathan with a fishhook or press down its tongue with a cord?" (Job 41:1).

"Of course we can," most answer. "With our modern equipment, we can kill all the crocodiles and whales if we want to."

Kill without limit—yes! Human beings have proven our ability to end life, but we have not shown that we can replace our Creator, nor escape God's judgment. The Book of Job tells us that God sets limits. An unlimited quest to dominate and destroy all independent life finds itself face-to-face with the living God.

From a biblical point of view, exemptionalism appears to be a radical form of hubris, pride. It attributes more power than we humans have, and it therefore overlooks the destructive consequences of our passionate commitment to ongoing growth and development. We may call ourselves *Homo sapiens*, but our knowledge is limited. Bound by the faithless actions of those who went before us, as well as denying scientific information about climate change, we are undone. Like rats lost in a maze we built ourselves, rather than bringing heaven's beautiful ordinances to earth, we are disordering the entire planet—indeed, *unmaking* God's creation.[4]

Necessity and the way things are precede, shape, and finally determine human life and institutions. Corporate prosperity is measured by the bottom line of profit and loss, but when we unmake creation to make a profit, we destabilize the ecological life systems to our own peril. Big houses, expensive cars, high status, membership at the right clubs—individual success cannot protect us from the doom that ripens in our quest for progress and development. The necessities of natural law cannot be ignored.[5]

Infinite growth of human populations, industries, farms, fisheries, and cities is impossible on a finite planet.[6] From whales to cod to menhaden, sooner or later, exploitive growth and development must end. If we know one thing about ecology, it is that no population of animals or plants increases forever. Disease, predators, and famine restore balance. Usually the given population continues at a reduced level, but sometimes the changes are so extreme that the creatures become extinct (for instance, mammoths at the end of the Ice Age). The very order of creation that produces whales and human beings restores ecological and social balance.

What happens when people ignore all limits and press on toward endless growth, riches, power, and glory, no matter who gets hurt? God says, "Cease to do evil and learn to do good while you still have time." And if we still refuse to listen to reason? Then the created order itself will limit our growth, and we will direct our power against ourselves. War and natural disasters will produce catastrophic loss of human and natural life. Losses go beyond imagination, and suffering will be unthinkable. Survivors will echo the cry of Job, "Why, Oh Lord, why did I live to see this day?"

Survivors Ask Who Is to Blame for a Disaster

Theologian David Wolfers said that the Book of Job carried monotheism to its closest possible encounter with reality. When Wolfers was a twelve-year-old boy attending public school in Sydney, Australia, his English teacher, Mr. Anderson, suggested that the first example of a novel was the Book of Job. Wolfers went home and read the book for the first time. He found the work (in the King James translation) to be full of irreconcilable obscurities and self-contradictions, which he attributed to his incapacity as a young reader. He went on to a successful career, until one day his fascination with Job matured into a decision. Wolfers quit work, delved more deeply into the Hebrew language, and moved to Israel. Crediting his Jewish mother and father with his initial love of the Hebrew language, he began a word-by-word translation of Job. Finally, after a lifetime of labor, he completed *Deep Things Out of Darkness* (the title taken from Job 12:22) but only got to see the blue line copy before he died.

The Book of Job resolves the problem of the apparent incompatibility between a fundamentally unjust universe, capable of inflicting untold pain on the innocent, and a fundamentally benevolent Creator. Based on textual evidence, Wolfers held that Job is an allegorical figure representing the people of Judah and King Hezekiah during the Assyrian conquests. He thinks it's possible that the prophet Isaiah crafted the book after the destruction of Samaria. Job is a veiled story of national disaster, the rupture of covenants between the tribal desert God and the chosen people, and the trial of Israel's faith in exile. Job's personal disaster, betrayal, and temptation are an effective disguise and vehicle for the true theme of the book.

> The true occasion for the writing of the Book of Job was as a contribution to a debate over the significance of the destruction of the kingdoms of Israel and Judah by successive Assyrian monarchs, with a particular emphasis on the spectacular injustice of the "punishment" of Judah at just that time when there reigned a virtuous king who "did that which was right in the eyes of the Lord, according to all that David, his father, had done" (2 Chronicles 29:2; 2 Kings 28:3).[7]

Alone, afflicted by disease, mourning the loss of his loved ones, seemingly unheard, Job asks to present his case to God. He believes that "in [God's] hand is the life of every living thing and the breath of every human being" (Job 12:10). Like Israel after Samaria's destruction by the Assyrians, like Africans dragged in chains from their homes, sweating in the bowels of a slave ship, Job cries out to God, "Why is light given to one who cannot see the way, whom God has fenced in? For my sighing comes like my bread, and my groanings are poured out like water. For the thing that I fear comes upon me, and what I dread befalls me" (Job 3:23-25).

My Union Theological Seminary professor Robert McAfee Brown once said that suffering caused by natural events was hardest to understand but easiest to accept, whereas suffering coming from human beings was easiest to understand but hardest to accept. If we cannot accept the suffering that comes to us, the pain is too much to bear. In chapters 3–37, Job and his counselors wrestle with the misery that has come to him. How can a good God allow such suffering to occur?

Eliphaz, Bildad, Zophar, and Elihu are Job's friends and counselors. After three days of silence in respect for his suffering, they speak: "Think now, who that was innocent ever perished? Or where were the upright cut off" (Job 4:7). What has come to Job must be chastening from the Almighty. Since God blesses the upright, Job must be to blame for what has happened to him![8]

Human beings find it almost impossible to admit that events beyond our understanding and control may happen to them. Instead, somebody must be to blame, to be accountable. Sometimes we feel that something is wrong with ourselves, like a child who has said angry words to a parent who then leaves the house and meets an untimely death. Job's friends, on the other hand, cast blame on him. "Suffering persons express either compassion and comfort or else contempt and bitterness" (contrast Job 16:2,20; 19:19,21 and 2 Corinthians 1:6).[9]

Job responds forcefully, "No doubt you are the people, and wisdom will die with you. But I have understanding as well as you; I am not inferior to you. Who does not know such things as these?" (Job 12:2-3). In God's hand is the life of every living thing (Job 12:10). Job has seen and understands providence (13:1), yet with him it is a fact that trouble has indeed come upon a righteous man. His counselors cannot make any sense of his suffering. Neither can he, which leads him to God: "But I would speak to the Almighty, and I desire to argue my case before God" (13:3; cf. 28:20-28).

God calls every human to love God with heart, soul, mind, and strength, and to love their neighbors as themselves. When we fall away from our Creator and Redeemer, we fall under a curse, suffer, and die (as Deuteronomy 30:11-20). God is self-revealed in word and deed, working through the created order and human life for freedom, justice, and peace on planet Earth. When we do God's truth, we are blessed.

When God's people repent and do justice, they will be established, says Deuteronomy and many other Scriptures, yet why, when God's people were led by righteous King Hezekiah, was Judah laid waste and more than two hundred thousand Judeans brutally driven into exile? Job, a righteous man, attributes such unmerited suffering to God:

> Even when I cry out, "Violence!" I am not answered.
> I call aloud, but there is no justice.
> He has walled up my way so that I cannot pass,
> and he has set darkness upon my paths.
> He has stripped my glory from me,
> and taken the crown from my head.
> He breaks me down on every side, and I am gone,
> he has uprooted my hope like a tree. —Job 19:7-10

How could God, who is good and all-powerful, allow Hezekiah and his people to be conquered? God, through Sennacherib, stripped Hezekiah of his honor and lifted the crown from his head. The Assyrian troops threw up their ramps to take the city (Job 19:12). Were the siege works around Jerusalem God's (Job 19:6)? Hezekiah's old friends abominated him, and his servants refused to answer his call. He escaped only "by the skin of his teeth" (19:20).

Sennacherib had a ready answer to why God allowed Judah to be overcome by Assyria. The Lord, indeed, had said to him, "Go up against this land and destroy it" (Isaiah 36:10). The commander of his great army proclaimed these chilling words to the Judeans assembled on the walls of Jerusalem:

> Do not let Hezekiah mislead you by saying, "The LORD will deliver us." Has any of the gods of the nations delivered their land out of the hand of the king of Assyria? Where are the gods of Hamath and Arpad? Where are the gods of Sepharvaim? Have they delivered Samaria out of my hand? Who among all the gods of these countries have delivered their countries out of my hand, that the LORD should deliver Jerusalem out of my hand? (Isaiah 36:18-20)

"My conquering power has no limit," said Sennacherib. Might, not right, reigns. The Lord of Israel is no different than any other god who cannot deliver. Job's illness is a metaphor for Assyria's ravages. The boils and sores predicted by Deuteronomy fall on the whole people, including their king (Deuteronomy 28:35).[10]

Understandings of covenant led many to the idea that a good man would earn a good life, as in the American prosperity gospel, whereas the end of the wicked would be disaster. Even today the American dream of economic success is undergirded by the conviction that honest, hard work leads to individual advancement. Ancient Israel, as today, understood that virtue conferred prosperity and immunity from the pitfalls of life. Job's counselors assert that he suffers because he is unrighteous. He should therefore repent, and God will restore him to health and prosperity.

For the Book of Job's author, however, the Assyrian conquest of Samaria and Judah rendered bankrupt the assumption that keeping God's covenant conferred prosperity. "Therefore the very survival of the Hebrew God, and by unavoidable corollary, the Israelite nation, was in jeopardy. A new and even more realistic foundation for the faith had become an urgent necessity."[11]

> So the Book of Job emerges as the record of the eliciting from the Jewish people of that genuine love of God which could never have been discovered or revealed as long as the covenantal relationship remained intact in unmodified form. It is a vital document in the history of religion, marking the first appearance of devotion as a free-will offering, and of the extension of the concept of the one national god to that of One God for all.[12]

God Opens the Book of Nature

God meets Job in the makeup of the created order. Physics, astronomy, chemistry, geology, biology, geography, and climatology reveal the characteristics of the universe in which we live. Though the concept of laws of nature may have fallen out of favor, the planet's structures and processes continue to determine existence. We still speak of earthquakes and hurricanes as acts of God, natural events beyond human control. Likewise, the processes of birth, growth, maturity, reproduction, aging, death, and recycling of nutrients are necessary. Humans are made from the earth's dust, to it we return, and the earth shapes our fate within the institutions and nations that our ancestors brought into being.

My friend and colleague in ministry Charles Yopst said,

> The resolution of suffering lies in compassion and hope and not in simplistic rational logic. The book of Job is about relationships rather than explanations and shows how the search for explanations clouds relationships. People can endure almost any suffering except the

> deprivation of hope. Love is shared hope. Compassion is the mother of hope. Hope multiplies energy and coordinates rhythms. God is the basis of hope.[13]

For thirty-eight chapters, Job and his friends struggle to understand and accept Job's anguish. Throughout all this time, Job remains seated on a garbage dump. We can imagine a modern Job upon Chicago's Mount Trashmore, an immense sanitary landfill. Elihu, in chapter 37, concludes his long address with God speaking through the storm:

> Listen! Hear well the turmoil of His voice,
> And the roar that issues from His throat!
> He unleashes it under the whole of the heaven,
> And His lightning to the corners of the earth,
> After it rumbles the voice.
> It thunders with the voice of His majesty,
> And none can outpace them, for His voice shall
> be heard![14]

Suddenly the Lord answers Job out of the depths of natural power—from the crashing thunder and shattering lightning. As Job struggles for existence, the One who laid the earth's foundations speaks through the rainstorms that birth life:

> Then the LORD answered Job out of the whirlwind:
> "Who is this that darkens counsel by words
> without knowledge?
> Gird up your loins like a man;
> I will question you, and you shall declare to me.
> Where were you when I laid the foundation of
> the earth?
> Tell me, if you have understanding." —Job 38:1-4

Then, the Lord takes Job to day one of Creation, that day before all days, that day present now in God's holy presence, that day toward which all creation moves. When the Spirit speaks, Job *knows* the One beyond all knowing. The speech that follows resonates with passion. It "is wholly at variance with every orthodox conception of the character of the Creator. The speech displays what the modern psychologist terms 'inappropriate affect.' The Lord, in a welter of sarcasm and abuse, sets out to diminish Job from his first words."[15]

Sarcasm comes from a Greek word meaning to tear flesh. It describes an ironic form in which the speaker is motivated by scorn. During the years I struggled to deal with my wife's paranoid dementia, I slowly learned that sarcastic words neither hurt nor controlled me when I realized that they were not about me. When I reacted in kind, my sarcastic words cut me down inside, as well as hurt my loved one. I prayed, "God, teach me to detach my mind from what others say and do, except to draw helpful lessons and guidance from them."[16]

David Wolfers wondered if the author of the Book of Job wished to portray a God afflicted by a sense of guilt toward Job, determined upon attack as the best form of defense, saying, "There is a brutality in the Lord's questions which belongs to the inquisitor, not his victim."[17] He concluded, however, "We may properly postulate that in this speech the Lord is acting a role as a participant in the debate (between Job and his friends), and that what appeals to us as unwarranted and brutal abuse may in fact be no more than a display of superior skill in a specialized medium of intercourse."[18]

The fear of the Lord is the beginning of wisdom. A healthy fear of danger is essential to survival. When we must protect ourselves and our loved ones, not being afraid is foolishness. The word *fear* comes from Old English *faer,* literally a sudden attack. A snare lifts a terrified animal into the air. An ambush surprises unsuspecting travelers. The predator lies in wait and leaps upon its prey. Fear means the feeling of anxiety and agitation caused by the presence of danger, evil, and pain, but it also means respectful dread, awe, and reverence.

Definitions of fear show a fascinating complexity. Terror and awe come from the same source in the human heart. Life brings into being ones who were not and then shapes and challenges us until we return to dust. Who has not sensed awe when reflecting on the mysterious, joyful wonder of life? All creatures must watch for threats to their existence and well-being. With our immense mental power to remember and foresee, we human beings often multiply fears into toxic states of uneasiness or panic that take us down.

Poured out on ancient Israel was the fury of war (Isaiah 42:25). Who could understand such burning suffering and loss? The prophet Isaiah asked, "Who handed Jacob over to become loot, and Israel to the plunderers? Was it not the LORD against whom we have sinned?" (42:24). A new era began. God broke the powers that held Israel in bondage. God's servants, therefore, do not have to be afraid, for we are redeemed from slavery. Like a litany, God said again and again, "Do not fear" (43:1,5; 44:2,8).

Declared the psalmist, "Holy and awesome is [God's] name. The fear of the LORD is the beginning of wisdom" (Psalm 111:9-10). Fear becomes holy awe when the Lord becomes our center of attention. Before "all God's waves and billows had gone over us," before we had been consumed by fire all around, but now the Lord, who created and formed Israel, says, "Do not fear, for I have redeemed you; I have called you by name; you are mine" (Isaiah 43:1).

As God speaks, Job's universe suddenly becomes immense, including sea, clouds, snow, and rain, even the stars of the Pleiades (38:8-38). The Lord's voice shifts Job's concentration from himself. Until God spoke, Job's place, time, and culture limited his understanding (as it does ours). Humans are ethnocentric—our race, class, and nation are central to the universe. We are also prone to thinking our species is the best. When disasters come, ruined cities, a conquered nation, and dead children leave survivors immersed in suffering. Illness shrinks a person's universe to the sick room. No one escapes the limits of time, place, and culture, even a truly righteous person like Job.[19] God's questions require prolonged and disciplined contemplation. Cosmic realities understood and shaped by the Creator become questions addressed to Job. "By the choice of their starting place, the divine speeches suggest that one understand human community and identity in the light of creation, rather than attempting to understand God and the cosmos on the basis of particular human social arrangements."[20]

To grasp what is said to Job, immersed in the modern industrial society's mentality as we are, we must recognize that shifting our attention from civilization to nature is monumental. We work inside enclosed factories and offices. Our recreation centers on sports done by professionals in human-made stadiums. When we go outside, we engage in activities like golf that occur in manicured settings and concentrate attention on improvement in numerical scores, or we jet ski, oblivious to what is below the waves. Our industrial civilization seems only to value an urban, computerized, consuming way of life, usually measured by the bottom line. "Does it make money?" Almost never outside, how could a voice from a storm make sense to us?

Suppose, like Job, we go outdoors to a dumping place abandoned by civilization, such as an abandoned strip mine or quarry, to hear, see, and reflect. As early Christian wilderness-dwelling monks taught, when we open the book of nature, we meet its Author.[21]

Some years ago, family troubles bound me. The more money, time, and effort I gave, the worse things got. When I began to see and talk about what was happening, the troubles really started! One Saturday morning, my first wife and I had an intense argument. I left the house and drove to West Valley Creek. After parking,

I walked to the stream, across a place where we sweated to restore a section of the creek, and climbed halfway up the opposite bank to an abandoned road. Above was a steep slope of broken rocks that surrounded the part of the quarry now filled by a lake.

No one was fishing that day. I was alone. Looking at the broken boulders, struggling plants, and dredged stream, I felt I was in the right spot. My life, too, was in shambles. I felt sad, depressed, and exhausted. I sat on a big stone, closed my eyes, breathed deeply, and prayed.

When I opened my eyes, a tiny yellow flower at my feet caught my attention. Beside it was a patch of emerald-green grass and blue cornflowers. Just as the stream was coming alive again in response to our restoration efforts, new life was springing into being.

A sound began to register: *Kuk-kuk, kuk-kuk!* My attention turned from marriage and family problems. The repetitive call got louder and closer. Still seated on the boulder, I twisted slowly and looked over my shoulder up the grassy slope. The grass moved—something was cautiously approaching. Suddenly a great bird stepped into full view. Its iridescent colors spoke of a cock pheasant, but it seemed bigger. As that cautious male bird revealed himself fully, my mind exploded: "No one is so fierce as to dare to stir . . . up [Leviathan]. Who can stand before it?" (Job 41:10). Immediately I felt power. If no tyrant could control creation or Creator, I was free. I, cautious like the great bird, could reveal myself and do what was right as best I could.

Memory Fades—Love Endures

Years after my second wife, Irene, entered Kendal's full-care nursing facility, I returned one night with dinner to where we once lived together. A poem came to me.

> Entering an empty room,
> on the wall Irene's photo of a tree in full autumn color,

alone, I miss her.
Though dementia swept memories away,
and past intimacies are gone,
caring nurses diminish her paranoid fears.
Hospital-short visits bring new delights,
a picture in an album, "Oh I remember that!"
Wheelchair walks in the sunshine,
seeing nature together as we've always done.
Memory fades—love endures,
"I love you, Irene, more than ever."
"I love you too, Owen!"

Scripture is generated by the presence of the living God, the source and sustainer of life. All creatures live by the Maker's sustaining grace (see Job 38:39-41; Matthew 6:25-34). Life comes to us through God's hands moment by moment, day by day. In the most literal, physical sense, we live by grace through faith. God, the Bible says, works in, with, and through all that is made. Just as within the natural order ecosystems move toward balance, we may use human capacities to balance our lives. Recognizing that we are trapped is the first step to sanity.

God invites us back into life from the human-caused crises that are destroying us. *Let go and let God*, says the Spirit's still, small voice. Stop being preoccupied with making, hurrying, and watching TV, and open yourself to the One who formed you. Confess the power jag you feel when cutting down another living being and release your controlling need to dominate. Acknowledge your limits. For one moment, stay within your body's boundaries. Look around and you will see God's natural creations, just as did the author of Job.

> [Leviathan] makes the deep boil like a pot;
> it makes the sea like a pot of ointment.

> It leaves a shining wake behind it;
> one would think the deep to be white-haired.
> On earth it has no equal,
> a creature without fear.
> It surveys everything that is lofty;
> it is king over all that are proud. —Job 41:31-34

Judging from what God said to Job, we may anticipate that God will not feel sorry for us, no matter how great our suffering. The Lord speaks to this suffering survivor in rough language: "Gird up your loins like a man; I will question you, and you declare to me" (Job 40:7). God approached Job in a way that respected him. He might be sick and bankrupt, but he was still a man who could gird up his loins and answer questions the Creator of the universe was about to address to him. Job was stronger than he thought![22]

As the Lord speaks to Job, one natural limit after another appears. "Where were you when I laid the foundation of the earth?" (Job 38:4). "Who shut in the sea with doors?" (38:8). "Have you commanded the morning?" (38:12). "Have the gates of death been revealed to you?" (38:17). The orders of creation are of worth in themselves and indeed provide the structures of human moral order.[23]

Wilderness provides a source of limits: "Can you hunt the prey for the lion?" (Job 38:39). "Do you know when the mountain goats give birth?" (39:1). "Who has let the wild ass go free?" (39:5). "Is it by your wisdom that the hawk soars?" (39:26). Within the created order established and maintained by the Lord, wild creatures live in balance.[24] "No one is so fierce as to dare to stir . . . up [Leviathan]. Who can stand before it?" (41:10).

Conclusion

Sing with all who survive losses, "Sometimes I feel like a motherless child." God brings us into a universe of love. Lift the survivor's question, "Who is to blame for the disaster?" Go to a natural place, and let God open the book of nature. Look up, and look around you. See the shining water and green leaf. Hear the quick-moving warbler. Release your life to your Creator. Feel the gift of life. Let delight in God's creation fill your soul. Join in the chorus of praise to the One who created and sustains every bird, plant, and whale.

> Give to the winds thy fears;
> hope and be undismayed.
> God hears thy sighs and counts thy tears,
> God shall lift up thy head.[25]

Hope begins and ends in prayer. Remember "In God's hand is the life of every living thing and the breath of all humankind" (Job 12:10). *You are alive. Give thanks and sing!*

Notes

1. As, e.g., in Robert Bellah, *The Broken Covenant* (Seabury, 1975).
2. Edward O. Wilson, *In Search of Nature* (Shearwater, 1996), 188.
3. Wilson, *In Search of Nature*, 189–90.
4. In a statement that could have been written today, church leaders from around the world gathered at the 1992 Rio de Janeiro UN Conference on the Environment reported that trends toward the ecology/justice crises had gotten worse: "Consumption of energy continues as though it were limitless in content and benign in effect. Many animal and plant species have been brought to extinction. Pollution of water, soil, and air is greater than ever. Desertification and deforestation accelerate. Vast sums for weapons and militarization continue to drain desperately needed resources, and the practice of the powerful to use local conflict for political and economic purposes, after the ending of East-West confrontation, has escalated. The burden of the debt of poor countries has become more and more stifling. Hunger afflicts more and more people, not only in Asia, Africa, and Latin America, but also in the Eastern European countries, the Middle East, the Far East, the Caribbean, and even within the affluent nations of the so-called 'First World.' Economic policies imposed upon already impoverished countries strangle the possibility of survival for multitudes of people. And the children, what shall we say to children and generations to come? We have come to the conclusion that

the prevailing system is exploiting nature and peoples on a worldwide scale and promises to continue at an intensified rate." World Council of Churches UNCED Group, *Searching for the New Heavens and the New Earth* (World Council of Churches, 1992).

5. Doris Lessing, *The Sirian Experiments* (Knopf, 1981), helps us understand necessity grounded in cosmic order.

6. "In its neglect of the rest of life, exemptionalism fails definitively. . . . The environmentalist vision, prudential and less exuberant than exemptionalism, is closer to reality. It sees humanity entering a bottleneck unique in history, constricted by population and economic pressures. In order to pass through to the other side, within perhaps 50 to 100 years, more science and entrepreneurship will have to be devoted to stabilizing the global environment. That can be accomplished, according to expert consensus, only by halting population growth and devising a wiser use of resources than has been accomplished to date. And wise use for the living world in particular means preserving the surviving ecosystems, micromanaging them only enough to save the biodiversity they contain, until such time as they can be understood and employed in the fullest sense for human benefit." Wilson, *In Search of Nature*, 198–99.

7. David Wolfers, *Deep Things Out of Darkness* (Eerdmans, 1995), 13–15, 64–70.

8. Several subthemes are repeated in similar literary sections by Eliphaz, Bildad, and Zophar (Scripture references respectively): (1) The end of the wicked is suffering and shame (4:9; 18:5; 20:4-9). (2) So God's wisdom permitting suffering is questioned only by the wicked (15:1-16; 25:1-6; 11:5-12). (3) And therefore all sufferers are to repent (22:1-30; 8:5-7,20,21; 11:13-19). According to Eliphaz, those good persons who suffer do so briefly and are purified (5:17). Wolfers, *Deep Things Out of Darkness*, 107–8.

9. Wolfers, *Deep Things Out of Darkness*, 1. "Job's three counselors substituted purifying for nurturing. They assumed that Job's misfortunes may contaminate them. They were sidetracked onto their own issues and clichés and agendas, projecting them onto Job, instead of soothing Job's sufferings." Charles G. Yopst, *Who Can Comfort Job? Meeting God Through Suffering* (unpublished document, 1999), 2.

10. "There is no reference in the poem of Job to any disease of the skin. It is almost as certain that there is no reference to physical disease of any kind. It is indeed striking that of the ten passages which are commonly translated in such a way as to support or convey the impression of illness, no fewer than eight have been able to achieve this result only by translating known Hebrew words in ways which do not correspond to any parallels within the corpus of biblical literature. The statistical probability that this is mere coincidence is effectively zero." Wolfers, *Deep Things Out of Darkness*, 131–32.

11. Wolfers, *Deep Things Out of Darkness*, 17.

12. Wolfers, *Deep Things Out of Darkness*, 208.

13. Yopst, *Who Can Comfort Job?*, 3. See also the Dalai Lama and Desmond Tutu, *The Book of Joy: Lasting Happiness in a Changing World* (Avery/Penguin Random House, 2016), 196–201.

14. Wolfers, *Deep Things Out of Darkness*, 17, Wolfer's translation.

15. Wolfers, *Deep Things Out of Darkness*, 208.

16. Al-Anon Family Group Headquarters, *One Day at a Time in Al-Anon* (2000), 7.

17. Wolfers, *Deep Things Out of Darkness*, 209, 211.

18. Wolfers, *Deep Things Out of Darkness*, 212.

19. "The way a person answers such questions is in large part a matter of the horizon of meaning within which a person thinks. The contrast between the horizon within which Job presents himself in chapters 29–31 and the horizon within which God asks Job to locate himself could not be sharper. Job's primary horizon of meaning was the village and the family. God challenges the parochialism of Job's moral imagination by making the starting point nothing less than the whole of creation." *The New Interpreter's Bible*, vol. IV (Abingdon, 1996), 625.

20. *The New Interpreter's Bible*, 626.

21. See Robert Gottfried and Frederick Kruger, *Living in an Icon: A Program for Growing Closer to Creation and to God* (Church Publishing, 2019).

22. *The Jewish Study Bible–Tanakh Translation*, ed. Adele Berlin and Marc Zvi Brettler (Oxford University Press, Jewish Publication Society, 1985, 1999). "The Book of Job as we have it makes three main points which are interrelated. The most obvious point is that human suffering is not necessarily deserved. This leads to the second point. The claim that all suffering is deserved will inevitably persuade those who hold that view to falsify either the character of the sufferer or the character of the Lord. The third point, however, is the most theologically difficult and gives the book its sense of profundity and at the same time its inconclusive conclusion. There is no way of understanding the meaning of suffering. That is, in the Lord's argument, the reasons for suffering—if there are any—are simply beyond human comprehension" (1500).

23. "The 'moral sense of nature' is above all an affirmation that the natural world has intrinsic value." *The New Interpreter's Bible*, vol. IV, 626.

24. *The New Interpreter's Bible*, vol. IV, 595.

25. Paul Gerhardt, "Give to the Winds Thy Fears," trans. John Wesley (public domain).

CHAPTER 9

Universe of Love

The Lord is gracious and merciful. No matter what we have done, said, and been, the One who formed us in our mothers' wombs still loves us. Scripture, like a pilgrim traveling through the ages, reminds every generation that the Source of life is like a loving parent. People went to hear the founder of Christianity, Jesus of Nazareth, because he preached good news of a loving God (Mark 1:14-15), lived his message by healing and freeing people, and died on a cross. He is present today to ransom us from sin. Our Lord and Savior walks with us as we pick up our own crosses, love our neighbors as ourselves, and follow him. When we turn to God, warm, tender love surrounds us, like a baby in his or her mother's arms. Then the Spirit's truthful light leads us through suffering and joy as we learn to do justice, love mercy, and walk humbly with God.

> *Use the intelligence and power I gave you to rescue the perishing and restore the earth!* —Your Creator

The Spirit meets us where we are strongest. Our shoulders carry a big head with a powerful mind. Our eyes see what's going on. Our ears hear life's sounds. Our nose picks up scents in the place we live. Our feet carry us where we want to go. Our hands touch, shape, create, and use tools. Indeed, our whole body radiates energy.

The Bible says we were formed to walk along our life's journey following signposts pointing toward living with our Creator: reverence for life, interdependence with life, stewardship of life, and integrity in life. When we meet living beings in need, like the Good Samaritan, we stop and help. When we see our planet's forests logged, burning, and dying, we give time, energy, and money to protect, preserve, and restore.

God is unconditional love. Underneath everything are God's everlasting arms. Indeed, our Creator holds planet Earth with love and care. Søren Kierkegaard said that believing in God is like wading out into the ocean on a calm day.[1] Further and further out you go until only your toes touch the bottom. Will you push off and swim into the unknown? That takes faith, believing in your ability to swim and God's upholding power.

When we decide to let go and let God, take our feet off the bottom, and swim, we become God's ministers. Through trusting the One who made us, God provides all we need. Knowing that all we have and are is entrusted to us by God, we are freed to share with others. We are free to use our time on earth building and restoring. God's promises throughout the sacred Scriptures assure us that God is in charge, no matter how dark the night. Just as those who went before us, we learn to heal and defend God's lands and waters, animals and plants, even as we do justice and proclaim good news to the poor.

The personal Source of life loves every one of us. "Take delight in the LORD, and he will give you the desires of your heart" (Psalm 37:4). Gracious love comes as a gift, a surprise, an unexpected fulfillment of our deepest desires and longings. God's love surrounds everyone. Indeed, the entire universe is created, sustained, and revitalized by the Lord's steadfast covenant love (Psalm 36:5-9). God heard cries of suffering, saw with compassion, came down to deliver, and sent Moses to free God's people from slavery in Egypt (Exodus 3:7-12). Likewise, Jesus said, "For the Son of Man came not to be served but to serve and to give his life as a ransom for many" (Mark 10:45). We are justified by grace through faith—that is the gospel promise (Romans 3:21-26).

Throughout the Scriptures, text after text tells us, "The LORD is gracious and merciful (as Psalm 111:4, or Luke 1:50-54).[2] The Hebrew adjective *rahum*, meaning merciful and gracious, is used only for the Creator throughout Scripture.

> "Yahweh merciful and gracious" belongs to recitals of the saving acts of God in history, acts freely given for individual and corporate liberation (Ps. 111:4, 145:8, Neh. 9:17). It is also found in individual petitions for deliverance (Ps. 86:16). It is motivation for national and divine repentance (Joel 2:13, 2 Chron. 30:9, Jonah 4:2) as well as for the unmerited forgiveness of sin, even in the presence of deceit, apostasy, rebellion, and hypocrisy (Ps. 78:38, 103:8). Again the merciful God restores after national defeat (Dt. 4:31) and sends blessings upon the righteous person (Ps. 112:4).[3]

In the Bible, the womb (*rehem*) is a physical organ of the body that suggests warm, tender love. Phyllis Trible says that a mother's love truly points like a finger to the Lord: "The womb protects and nourishes but does not possess and control. It yields its treasure in order that wholeness and well-being may happen. Truly it is the way of compassion."[4]

In Scripture, moreover, the wombs of women belong to God:

> God conceives in the womb; God fashions in the womb; God judges in the womb; God brings forth from the womb; God receives out of the womb; and God carries from the womb to gray hairs. From this uterine perspective, then, Yahweh molds life for individuals and for the nation Israel. Accordingly in Biblical traditions an organ unique to the female becomes a vehicle pointing to the compassion of God.[5]

Sorrow, as well as joy, comes to all life. Loss of income, housing, and freedom may fall upon us, but hardest to bear is the death of loved ones, particularly our children. "Thus says the LORD, A voice is heard in Ramah, lamentation and bitter weeping. Rachel is weeping for her children; she refuses to be comforted for her children, because they are no more" (Jeremiah 31:15).

From her grave, Israel's ancestral mother cries out, weeping, "Oh—not one here!" As Trible reflects, "Directed to no one in particular, and hence to all who may hear, the voice of Rachel travels across the land and through the ages to permeate existence with a suffering that not even death can relieve (see Matthew 2:18)."[6]

The soldier may see a dead enemy, or "collateral damage," a lifeless civilian beside the road, but Rachel weeps, refusing to be consoled for her children. Not a few abandon their ancestral faith because they cannot see how a loving God allows such terrible things. It is so hard to bear, nourish, and educate a child. Why, indeed, does God make it so easy to kill?[7]

The Lord is gracious and merciful. Cries of women and children are heard. "Thus says the LORD: Keep your voice from weeping and your eyes from tears, for there is a reward for your work, says the LORD: they shall come back from the land of the enemy; there is hope for your future, says the LORD: your children shall come back to their own country" (Jeremiah 31:16-17).

The prophets call those with power, influence, and money to care for the most vulnerable. The source of biblical justice—the power that motivates the prophets—is God, who hears the cries of all generations' Rachels. God's consoling voice addresses the suffering woman personally: *your* voice, *your* eyes, *your* work, *your* future, *your* children.

As Thomas Moore penned,

> Come, ye disconsolate, where'er ye languish,
> Come to the mercy seat, fervently kneel.

Here bring your wounded hearts, here tell your anguish;
Earth has no sorrow that heav'n cannot heal.[8]

God's concern for Rachel leads to consideration for her children. "Truly I have heard Ephraim rocking in grief" (Jeremiah 31:18, Trible's translation). For generations men were taught to survive in a world of empires. They learned to take orders, be hard and goal-oriented, and turn their eyes away from the "collateral damage" done to women, children, and the earth. An empire expands and maintains itself one war after another. Men try to drown their suffering caused by working, fighting, and drinking.

Rachel's child, Ephraim—another name for the people of God—discovered another way. He repented, turned from the way of death to the way of life, and opened himself again to the One who created and sustained him: "You disciplined me, and I took the discipline; I was like an untrained calf. Bring me back; let me come back, for you are the LORD my God. For after I had turned away I repented, and after I was discovered, I struck my thigh; I was ashamed, and I was dismayed because I bore the disgrace of my youth" (Jeremiah 31:18-19). Every woman, every man, every being is precious to the Lord: "Is Ephraim my dear son? My darling child? For the more I speak of him, the more do I remember him. Therefore my womb trembles for him; I will truly show motherly compassion on him. Oracle of Yahweh" (Jeremiah 31:20).[9]

"The human mother refuses consolation; the divine Mother changes grief into grace. As a result, the poem has moved from the desolate lamentations of Rachel to the redemptive compassion of God."[10]

Joy of the desolate, light of the straying,
Hope of the penitent, fadeless and pure.
Here speaks the Comforter, tenderly saying,
"Earth has no sorrow that heav'n cannot cure."[11]

Delivered from the Pit

When all seems hopeless, and we cry for help, God delivers us from the pit of tumult and sets our feet on solid rock (Psalm 40:1-2). The womb-like love of God surrounds everybody, men included, but we men can be really dense. We love our mothers, wives, and daughters and want what is best for them. We know, deep inside, that every human is created in God's image, different but equal. Yet, like all sinners, we want the world to revolve around our desires, interests, social position, and passions: "I'm a man. Do what I want. Feed me. Have sex with me. Make me happy!"

Nobody can live without love. A fancy car, a big house, fame, fortune, and imperial power are barren without love. Even the hard-driving man suddenly stops short when a woman's warm, loving hand touches him.

The world is cold and cruel, but a gracious and merciful God is in control. God saves many through their mother's love. In war, men dragged down by drink and caught up in wild living remembered their mother prayed for them, and that helped pull them through. After a hard, dark year in New York City, away from home and family, I recall coming back for Christmas. When I told Mother about my failures at seminary, she said, "Owen, I still love you."

The Hebrew word *tamrurim* in Jeremiah 31:15 means bitterness, but in 31:21 it means guideposts. Despair becomes hope. And hope points the way to a new future! Suddenly the male Ephraim becomes a daughter, Israel: "How long will you waver, O faithless daughter? For the Lord has created a new thing in the land: female surrounds man" (Jer. 31:22; Trible's translation).

Virile adult male is surrounded by female:

> Accordingly, female surrounding man is Rachel the mother embracing her sons with tears and with speech; it is Yahweh consoling Rachel about Ephraim; it is the daughter Israel superseding the son, Ephraim. And it is more

> than these images. Female surrounding man has power to dry up the tears of Rachel; to fulfill the compassion of Yahweh and to overturn the apostasy of Israel. And it is other than all these images, for it is Yahweh's creation of a new thing in the land. In short it is the poem itself.[12]

The form and content of Jeremiah's poem embody a womb. Who would not want to be loved again the way we were in our mother's womb? We know we cannot go back, even as Nicodemus pointed out to Jesus (John 3:1-21). And yet with God, all things are possible. "Woman encloses man. The female organ nourishes, sustains, and redeems the male child Ephraim."[13]

We experience true love when we open ourselves to being loved. John Wesley, Methodism's founder, believed in Christ and tried to do everything Jesus taught, starting a "holy club" at Oxford University, but he remained a sad and troubled man. One day he was at a worship service where the leader read from Paul's Letter to the Romans that we are justified by God's grace through faith. At once Wesley felt his heart was strangely warmed as he experienced God's love for him.

Soon he discovered that instead of feeling judged by God's commandments, they became a source of love and hope. We can make this world a better place to live, John Wesley taught. God is perfect in love, and therefore it is possible to be a loving person in this world. For Wesley, Christian perfection was not about keeping all the rules so you could go to heaven. Instead, he stressed Jesus' teaching that you and I can be more whole, complete, and perfectly loving in our daily lives. "I say to you: Love your enemies and pray for those who persecute you, so that you may be children of your Father in heaven, for he makes his sun rise on the evil and on the good, and sends rain on the righteous and on the unrighteous. . . . Be perfect, therefore, as your heavenly Father is perfect" (Matthew 5:44-45,48).

God judges, ends destructive ways, and is birthing a more ecologically whole and relationally just earth. Being made whole by God's love is more practical than other alternatives!

> Here see the bread of life, see waters flowing
> Forth from the throne of God, pure from above.
> Come to the feast of love; come, ever knowing
> Earth has no sorrow but heav'n can remove.[14]

Despite all we have done, taken, and said, there is a way back home. Jeremiah calls us to run back to mothering God's arms. The Lord is gracious and merciful. Grief-stricken Rachel's cries are heard. The merciful One says, *My womb-like love surrounds you. Go back to where you came from and start over, clean and fresh as a new day.*

Building Life on a Rock-Solid Foundation

God became incarnate in Jesus of Nazareth, whom we Christians worship as Lord and Savior:

- A first-century Jewish boy who grew up in a multicultural, mixed-race Galilean village where order was maintained by the oppressive Roman superpower
- A prophet who trusted in a steadfast, loving God, who preached and taught good news that despite oppression and evildoing, the Lord ruled
- A merciful, kind man who healed sick people and was comfortable walking among poor and homeless persons
- A Spirit-led person who, just as Moses led Israel out of slavery, went to the political and religious center of his country, Jerusalem, to give his life as a ransom for many

Like a modern mestizo person, Jesus from Galilee was an "insider-outsider" with closeness to and distance from his parent cultures and was able to see and appreciate characteristics in diverse groups, which served to shape him.[15] Jesus served God by helping people. He came out of his vision quest in the wilderness with a message of blessing: "The time is fulfilled, and the kingdom of God has come near; repent, and believe in the good news" (Mark 1:15). For him, being a servant of God meant releasing the Creator's life-giving and restoring power. Going back to his hometown synagogue in Nazareth, he turned the scroll to Isaiah 61:1-2 and 58:6 and read his goals for ministry (Luke 4:16-21). Anointed by the Spirit of the Lord, he set out to accomplish these goals:

- Preach good news to the poor.
- Proclaim release to the captives and recovery of sight to the blind.
- Set at liberty those who are oppressed.
- Proclaim the acceptable year of the Lord.

"Today this scripture is fulfilled in your hearing," said Jesus (Luke 4:21), reaffirming God's redemptive messages from Exodus. God's love reaches to the human pyramid's bottom, to those who are poor, mournful, humble, and hungry (Luke 6:20-21). Also blessed are those who intentionally enter the prophets' path—those who hunger and thirst for righteousness and are merciful, pure in heart, and peacemakers, and are persecuted for righteousness' sake.

The way Jesus lived with people shows that God loves us. He healed people, declaring God's forgiveness of their sins as he healed them. In memorable sayings and parables, he taught how to enter the way of life. Praying and meditating outdoors in the world God formed informed all Jesus said and did. As prophets before him, he said no to greed, destructive practices, and institutions, and yes to all that blessed and built up, warning of Judah's coming catastrophe if people did not repent and believe. In addition to healing, teaching, and preaching, Jesus organized and called disciples to live and minister with him. He poured out his life, serving and blessing through his words and deeds. At the end, he was oppressed and afflicted, wounded for our transgressions, and crushed for our iniquities. Raised from the dead by God, the Suffering Servant leads us into the way of peace.

Unlike imperial authorities' booming proclamations, the Servant's authority was communicated quietly—violent and coercive words were left to the tyrants (Isaiah 42:2). The poor and helpless were the crushed reed and fading wick that the Servant would neither break nor quench (42:3). Israel needed the blessings of pursuing justice, having mercy, and walking humbly with God, as does everyone.

The words given to the Servant to proclaim are amazing, and he would "faithfully bring forth justice" (Isaiah 42:3). Like the surging river seen by Amos, justice would flow, and the Servant would not grow faint or be crushed until he established justice in the earth. The coastlands awaited his teaching (42:3-4). The scope of revelation was broadened to include the nations, even the most remote regions Israelites knew, the coastlands. As did Moses to Israel, the Servant brought God's blessing to all people.

God's Servant Jesus not only came to teach and heal, but also to directly release the Creator's life-giving, restoring power, as in the story of Zacchaeus (Luke 19:1-10). Zacchaeus heard Jesus, acted on his words, and was saved. Salvation does not mean getting rich at others' expense. Precisely the opposite—being saved means rejoining God's family by making financial amends to those you hurt. Modern societies may separate family life from economic corporate life and forget about Creation's natural order, but Jesus meets us on the street and in our homes, talks in sensible ways about how we can be saved, and rejoices with us when we do what he says.

Being saved is a divine act, God's miracle. God delivers us from self-destructive words and deeds that harm others. Saved people work for the well-being of self and others, guided by God's commandments (especially the Sermon on the Mount and the Decalogue). When one is saved, often the entire household or corporate structure is touched, as happened with Zacchaeus. The lost are found!

Faith, hope, and love abide through all generations. Jeremiah showed us the Lord's power to regenerate all who repent. God set up a new covenant in Christ that offers hope and power. Raised from the dead and alive today, Jesus leads us forward as we pick up our own crosses and follow him. As we follow, filled with the sevenfold gifts of the Spirit, we join Abraham, Moses, Miriam, and the great company of witnesses. The Ten Commandments continue to bless and keep us, as Jesus reminded us in the Sermon on the Mount.[16]

In Genesis 1, the Creator of heaven and earth made humankind in God's image and gave them dominion over living creatures. On his final journey to Jerusalem, Jesus defined for his followers the meaning of dominion: *service*:

> You know that among the gentiles those whom they recognize as their rulers lord it over them, and their great ones are tyrants over them. But it is not so among you; instead, whoever wishes to become great among you must be your servant, and whoever wishes to be first among you must be slave of all. For the Son of Man came not to be served but to serve and to give his life as a ransom for many. (Mark 10:42-45)

Christ's life, death, resurrection, and living express life-giving service, as Paul reminded us in Philippians 2:1-10. When God's people relate to any living creature, we are there as life givers, Christ's stewards, and ministers. In the Bible, those who repent enter the narrow gate, and turn from death to life (Matthew 7:13-14). What is the gate to the way of life? Jesus said in Mark 10:45,

"The Son of Man came not to be served but to serve and to give his life as a ransom for many." The key word here is *ransom*, which in Greek (*lutpon*) means manumission from slavery. Not by creating servitude but instead freeing for service is the life-giving way. Jesus opens the life gate by giving his life.

We can understand what Jesus meant by *ransom* by reviewing the biblical texts upon which he drew. Clearly, he was guided by Isaiah's suffering servant passages in Isaiah 53:4-6:

> Surely he has borne our infirmities
> and carried our diseases,
> yet we accounted him stricken,
> struck down by God, and afflicted.
> But he was wounded for our transgressions,
> crushed for our iniquities;
> upon him was the punishment that made us whole,
> and by his bruises we are healed.
> All we like sheep have gone astray;
> we have all turned to our own way,
> and the LORD has laid on him
> the iniquity of us all.

The Servant's suffering and death open the gate to free, joyful living in God's kingdom. To see what this passage means, we must hear Jesus' explanation of what it does not mean: tyranny. Doing God's will does not mean lording it over, nor exercising authority over others (Mark 10:42). The wide way to destruction promises that if we beat down others to make them do what we want or kill them to get them out of our way, we will live free and happy lives. Jesus said that idea is false.

The political leadership norm in the ancient Near East was the *melek*, the all-dominant and majestic king. Samuel described how this institution would be established in Israel and how the king would make people work for his economic and political benefit (1 Samuel 8:10-18). The people wanted victory at any price. They became victims of their leader because they rejected the Lord as king over Israel (8:7). The kingdom split because free people would not tolerate King Rehoboam's tyranny forced upon them (1 Kings 12:16).

David was a wonderful poet whose psalms still inspire. A charismatic leader, he built a powerful nation, establishing an institution of authoritarian rule in Israel, supposedly God-sanctioned. Jesus' disciples wanted to link him with David, as did his time's Zealot freedom movement. Yet Jesus called himself the Son of Man, not Son of David. Why? To deliver his people from oppression, David took the way of war. When he succeeded, he said that God gave him the power to kill his enemies:

> You made my enemies turn their backs to me,
> and those who hated me I destroyed.
> They cried for help, but there was no one to save them;
> they cried to the LORD, but he did not answer them.
> I beat them fine, like dust before the wind;
> I cast them out like the mire of the streets.
> —Psalm 18:40-42

Jesus intentionally rejected the Davidic way of conquest, empire, and "divinely sanctioned" rule. God's purposes in this world will not be advanced by military conquest as described in Psalm 18. Peaceful ends cannot be separated from the means used to achieve them.

Power, rule, and glory on earth belong to God, despite the words Satan tested Jesus with: "All these [kingdoms of the world] I will give you, if you will fall down and worship me" (Matthew 4:9). "Worship the Lord your God, and serve only him," replied Jesus (verse 10). Only the One beyond all human naming and power is to be worshipped.

The image of ransom as liberation from slavery opens an additional dimension of Jesus' self-sacrifice: the true meaning of victory over evil, enacted in Jesus' healings and exorcisms. The One who freed the Hebrew people from Egyptian slavery becomes our deliverer in the Lord's chosen Servant. Those who specialize in building human and stone pyramids have lost their supposed power forever, not only in eternity but also in history.

Jesus' Galilean identity and his journey to Jerusalem are the starting points of Christian identity and mission today. "The poor will not be liberated from their misery by becoming wealthy but by discovering the new image of humanity now possible in Jesus. If the church is to be a faithful witness of the Master, it must be identified with the poor and oppressed of the world."[17] At Pentecost, Jews and proselytes from all nations heard in their own languages Spirit-filled people speaking of God's powerful deeds. When Peter spoke, not only did he cut to the heart with his message of the necessity for repentance and baptism, starting what was to become the Christian church, but he also said that these words are for us today: "For the promise is for you, for your children, and for all who are far away, everyone whom the Lord our God calls to him" (Acts 2:39).

Because Jesus frees, heals, and saves, emanating the Creator's life-generating energies, we, like the first disciples, are called by the Spirit of the living God to follow him. The Lord is shaping a new creation today, for the body of Christ is a multicultural microcosm of healing, environmental justice, peace, and love, embodying God's intent for the world.

How do Christian congregations become what God intends Christ's church to be, intentionally diverse and inclusive (racially, culturally, economically, in ability, and gender/sexual orientation)? Out of our histories of being oppressed and oppressing, new light is dawning. Vergilio Elizondo said,

> The task should be to see, critically and unemotionally, with insight and respect, what is truly humanizing and dehumanizing in each cultural tradition, and try to shape the new cultural identity by pulling together the best elements of each and reducing the harmful elements of each. It is the traditionally dominant group that will have to have the greater humility to face itself openly and admit that it has much to receive, much to learn, from the groups it has previously considered inferior. There is no question of one group "winning" over the other, but of all groups being willing to die a bit to their own egotism and ethnocentrism for the sake of the new creation.[18]

Many are cold, sick, hungry, thirsty, and oppressed. They cry, "Lift me up, feed me, help me!" Whole species of creatures facing extinction cry for help in like manner. We can build our lives upon this rock—faith in one loving God. Christians believe that when we accept Jesus Christ as our Lord and Savior, God's Son ransoms us from sin, and heals us and helps us walk the narrow way of everlasting life. Our task is to proclaim the good news to all nations, calling people to repent and believe in the gospel (Acts 3:11–4:12; 1 Corinthians 1:18-31), following Christ in loving service (Matthew 25:31-46; Romans 12:9-21).

The way Jesus called and taught his disciples shows how God uses life's sufferings to release constructive power. He began by proclaiming, "The time is fulfilled, and the kingdom of God has come near; repent, and believe in the good news" (Mark 1:15). The disciples listened and followed him. As Simon and Andrew immediately discovered, for Jesus, being in God's kingdom meant serving. Jesus healed a man with an unclean spirit, lifted Simon Peter's mother-in-law from a sickbed, and cured many others of disease (Mark 1:21-24).

The way we religious people often live, however, seems to deny that the universe is in God's loving hands. I hear you saying, "You 'people of God' fight with each other, persecuting and killing those who don't hold your beliefs; and you've also supported the war against nature. What about the Muslim wars of conquest, Christian crusades, genocide of native peoples of the Americas in the name of Christ, the Ku Klux Klan, or the Holocaust? Who'd want to join up with 'people of God' like you?"

As light shines into our lives and we begin to see what is happening to us, our task in religion—as in all life—is to learn our own guilt and repent—turn from the way of death to the Creator and Savior of heaven and earth. The Apostles' Creed highlights the conviction of Christians that Jesus Christ is both Lord and Savior. Past, present, and future rest in the righteous, powerful hands of God. Salvation is personal and social, occurs on this earth, and puts us on the way to everlasting life.[19] Repenting is like driving down a superhighway. On a big, modern road, you can get where you are going fast. But suppose you go in the wrong direction! The harder and faster you drive, the farther you get from the place you want to go. Instead, you must turn around and head toward your destination.

"Overcome evil with good," said Paul. The first step to everlasting life is hearing God's call and turning to enter God's life-giving way (Matthew 5–7). Those who commit to finding and walking the way of life are tempted to seek salvation and meaning in money, power, and fame, as was Jesus (Matthew 4:1-11). People of God, however, learn to know the one God and live by these divine commandments:

- Put the Lord first—not money, power, and fame.
- Be healers—not killers.
- Use kindness—not hatred.

- Do good—not evil.
- Be helpers—not dictators.
- Speak truth—not distort, ignore, deny, lie.
- Live in warm light—not darkness.
- Be givers—not takers.
- Be part of the solution—not the problem.

The second step to everlasting life is apprenticing, living with and learning from a spiritual leader who speaks truth and does the things that create a constructive state of well-being, peace on earth (*shalom*). Apprenticing involves trial-and-error learning. Speaking publicly, healing, dialoguing with friends and enemies, praying and meditating, feeding hungry people—these acts of faith are learned by being with someone who is doing the truth. As Jesus' disciples followed him, they learned from their errors, faults, even betrayals.

Third, trial-and-error learning results in keeping the focus on oneself, self-watching (as in Matthew 7:1-5). Being with Jesus led to frequent shocks of self-awareness, as when Peter's insight that Jesus was the Messiah was immediately followed by Jesus' adamant rejection while walking toward Jerusalem and calling Jerusalem and Rome to change their ways. Peter knew that would lead to suffering (Mark 8:31–9:1).

The fourth step for those who turn to the Lord for deliverance from evil is to speak and do the truth. When fearful, betraying Peter was addressed with empowering forgiveness, he was transformed. The "uneducated and ordinary" man who had denied Jesus three times a few weeks later stood before the highest religious council of his people and said, "Whether it is right in God's sight to listen to you rather than to God, you must judge; for we cannot keep from speaking about what we have seen and heard" (Acts 4:19-20).

Conclusion

These are dark times, and they seem to be getting darker as we listen to the news. God calls servants to reach out with words and deeds to people who are in desperate trouble, calling them to return to God and live. Think of a time when you were inside a dark building such as a barn. You could see dimly. Then you opened a door and stepped out into the sunshine and the light hurt your eyes. It was so bright you couldn't see. As your eyes became accustomed to the light, you saw shapes and colors—beauty everywhere.

God's steadfast love lets the light shine into our lives, and then we see. What is hurting people, community, river, church, trees, country? Right now, Jesus calls us in these times of crisis to be agents of light and liveliness.

Notes

1. A paraphrase of Søren Kierkegaard's *Leap of Faith.*

2. "If the concept of unity dominates the mind, it is the principle of compassion that governs the heart in Islam. Compassion is to oneness what radiance is to the sun: It is through compassion that the oneness of God most brilliantly shines forth and reveals its fundamental nature. Since compassion stems from oneness, it not only radiates, it also integrates; it exerts a merciful attraction upon all outward multiplicity: 'My Mercy encompasses all things'" (Koran 7:156). Reza Shah-Kazemi, *My Mercy Encompasses All: The Koran's Teachings on Compassion, Peace, and Love* (Counterpoint, 2007), 3.

3. Phyllis Trible, *God and the Rhetoric of Sexuality* (Fortress, 1978), 38.

4. Trible, *God and the Rhetoric of Sexuality*, 33. Men also participate in this metaphor of compassion in the Bible, as with Joseph for his brothers (Genesis 43:30), or in Psalm 103:13: "As a father has compassion for his children, so the LORD has compassion for those who fear him."

5. Trible, *God and the Rhetoric of Sexuality*, 38.

6. Trible, *God and the Rhetoric of Sexuality,* 40.

7. Hearing about what was happening in Europe during World War II, Abraham Heschel cried out, "There has never been more reason for man to be ashamed than now. Silence hovers mercilessly over many dreadful lands. The day of the Lord is a day without the Lord. Where is God? Why dost Thou not halt the trains loaded with Jews being led to slaughter? It is so hard to rear a child, to nourish and to educate. Why dost Thou make it so easy to kill? Like Moses, we hide our face, for we are afraid to look upon Elohim, upon His power of judgment.

Indeed, where were we when men learned to hate in the days of starvation? When raving madmen were sowing wrath in the hearts of the unemployed?" Abraham Heschel, *Moral Grandeur and Spiritual Audacity*, ed. Susannah Heschel (Farrar, Straus, and Giroux, 1996), 209–10.

8. Thomas Moore, "Come, Ye Disconsolate" (1816, public domain).

9. Phyllis Trible's translation in *God and the Rhetoric of Sexuality*, 45.

10. *God and the Rhetoric of Sexuality*, 46.

11. Moore, "Come, Ye Disconsolate."

12. Trible, *God and the Rhetoric of Sexuality*, 50.

13. Trible, *God and the Rhetoric of Sexuality*, 50.

14. Moore, "Come, Ye Disconsolate."

15. Virgilio Elizondo, *Galilean Journey: The Mexican American Promise* (Orbis, 2000), 18.

16. Manfred T. Brauch, *Set Free to Be You and Me* (Judson, 1975).

17. Elizondo, *Galilean Journey*, 93.

18. Elizondo, *Galilean Journey*, 27.

19. "I find perilous a proposition that pervades much of Christian culture in the United States. It asserts that Christianity, by its very nature, is concerned exclusively with the relation of the soul to eternity, the individual with God; that in the societal area the essential realization religion should provide is the worthlessness of human expectations of a better life on earth. The Son of God, we are told, took our flesh not to relieve our suffering but to forgive our sins. The thesis does violence to Scripture. Those who read in the sacred text a sheerly personal, individualistic morality have not understood the Torah, have not sung the Psalms, have not been burned by the prophets, have not perceived the implications and the very burden of Jesus' message, and must inevitably play fast and loose with St. Paul." Walter Burghardt, *Long Have I Loved You: A Theologian Reflects on His Church* (Orbis, 2000), 167.

CHAPTER 10

Going Home

At the end of a visit with Irene, she often says, "Take me home!" I, too, wish we could go back home to when we were younger and stronger. Who would not want to go back where we were known and loved? Yet times change. Where we were born is different from what it was, sometimes better, sometimes worse. When we turn to the living God, Scripture tells us we return to an everlasting home, right now and forever.

Returning to My Hometown

After Irene had a ministroke, Irene's daughter Amy and I arranged for Irene to go to Kendal's part-care facility, Cumberland, hoping she would recover. We planned that she would spend four nights there and then two or three at home. The first time I visited her, however, she grabbed me as I opened the door and tried to force her way out. A nurse hurried over and kept her from leaving. "I want to go home. I want to go home," she moaned. Feeling cut to my heart, I wanted to take her with me to our cottage, but I knew there was no way she could get the care she needed. After we moved Irene to our full-care facility, Westmoreland, and she spent a week at Chestnut Hill Hospital getting her medications adjusted, her paranoid fears diminished somewhat. Yet at every visit's end came her plea, "I want to go home!"

My earliest memories are of being in a home surrounded by love. Daddy and Mother, Grandma and Grandpa took care of me and let me know I was special to them, a wanted child. My first word was celebrated, and the event was recorded in my baby book. A picture taken on my first birthday shows me standing with my grandfather next to the kitchen stool, which held a magnificent angel-food cake Mother had baked for me. As I grew a little older, I loved to hear the story of my birth at the Fort Atkinson hospital in Wisconsin. I always connected being appreciated and loved with being devoted to God. Someday I would be a minister, a servant of God.

During the Second World War, we lived in Cambria, Wisconsin, and then in 1946, we moved back to "The Fort" so that my brother and I could get a good education. The Methodist church, public schools, the library, and the Rock River were places that formed and informed me. We fished the river, catching catfish, white bass, and sometimes walleye pike. We swam in Rock Lake and Lake Ripley. Uncle Andrew and Aunt Minnie owned a farm in Whitewater, through which a native trout stream flowed and from which I caught my first trout. When we visited, we took chickens and eggs home. This was a fertile land. Before 1946 almost all food was organic (before herbicides, pesticides, and antibiotic-fed cattle, pigs, and chickens). Milk and meat came from the farms, and we grew potatoes, corn, beans, and lettuce in our garden.

My parents', grandparents', and our church's faith allowed questions of meaning and truth. I owe an unrepayable debt to my teachers and those who reared me. In high school, I was taught to think by men and women dedicated to the life of the mind. On the Rock River and Lake Koshkonong, I discovered the delights of fishing, and with the sport I learned to love the natural realities of lake, forest, and meadow. The father of my childhood friend Ken, Norman Wittlief, told stories of huge northern pike he caught in the lake and showed us ducks he shot before he cleaned them. We begged him to take us fishing with him, but he replied, "Storms come up fast, and the waves get big. You are too little to fish Lake Koshkonong."

I always wondered about Koshkonong, the name of the big, shallow body of water. We knew the name was Native American and were aware of the many mounds they made long ago. Collectors sought arrowheads and found many after fields were plowed. The Native people called this big lake Koshkonong, "the one who feeds us." Scooped out by a glacier, it was a marshy lake, shallow, filled with wild rice. Waterfowl darkened the sky when frightened into flight by a cruising eagle. For more than ten thousand years, one Native American civilization after another followed the one before it. Each civilization shaped the environment with human purposes in mind, particularly when, in the spring, people burned the prairies to maintain the open savannas once characteristic of southern Wisconsin. For thousands of years, land and water remained fertile, abounding in fish, birds, and animals.

When we took my mother, Viola's, ashes back to our family cemetery plot, I did not expect to be connected with Native American ancestors also buried in my hometown. When I took a copy of my book *Living Waters* to the Fort Atkinson library as a gift of appreciation for all I had read there, the librarian thanked me and said, "You should read *The Mounds of Koshkonong and Rock River*, by Fort Atkinson historian Hugh Highsmith." When I did, I learned that where I grew up was a center of Native American life back to the last glacial period. I was unsurprised. Everyone in "The Fort" knew about Black Hawk and the Indian wars generated by white settlement, but we never studied these matters in school. Maybe we dimly knew that if we looked at our origins, we must change the way we thought and lived.

When my brother, Irene, and I took Mother's ashes to Evergreen Cemetery where Grandma, Grandpa, and Dad are buried, it looked like it did when I was in high school. Every Memorial Day the high school band marched up Main Street to this cemetery where the men who fought and died to save the Union are buried. We played the national anthem when we reached the center of

Evergreen Cemetery, and I remember my classmate, Harry Gutermuth, reading Lincoln's Gettysburg address as the gathered crowd stood silently.

In the 1820s, Wisconsin was a new frontier: "Settlers started coming onto the Sauk and Fox lands in 1823 to claim the land promised by the treaties. They tried to force the Indians to move across the Mississippi by destroying their crops, burning their lodges, insulting the women and mistreating the men. After a winter hunt in 1830, the tribe returned in the spring to find Sakenuk taken over by whites and their graveyard plowed into fields."[1] Keokuk, chief of the Sacs, gave in to government pressure and moved across the Mississippi. Black Hawk went along but returned to his homeland in 1832. Carrying flags of truce, three of a small band of warriors approached the army led by Isaiah Stillman. They were shot and killed by the militiamen! The remaining warriors then took cover and routed the unorganized cavalry.

With four hundred warriors, six hundred women and children, sixty-five-year-old Black Hawk decided to fight the white invasion. He attacked frontier settlements in Wisconsin and Illinois, killing more than two hundred white people between May 14 and July 31, 1832. General Henry Atkinson led a four thousand–man army to find and defeat Black Hawk. Traveling through difficult terrain, they arrived at Lake Koshkonong to find that Black Hawk had moved north. General Atkinson built a fort on the Rock River on July 11, 1832, which he called Fort Koshkonong, later renamed Fort Atkinson in his honor. It was hard to feed the army, so Atkinson released many soldiers, including Private Abraham Lincoln.

The Sauks fled from Rock Lake to the Four Lakes (now the site of the capital, Madison), and then to where the cavalry overtook them on the Wisconsin River's banks. In this battle, sixty-eight warriors were killed and many wounded, while the whites lost only one. The next day, Black Hawk tried to surrender, but no one in the army understood Sauk or Winnebago (which the messenger spoke). Besides, the army was motivated by a clear sense of purpose—get rid of the Indians! A gunboat with a six-pound cannon fired into the tribe. Colonel Grenville M. Dodge's infantry came up from behind. The Sauk were driven into the water. After three hours of slaughter, at least 150 were killed and the same number drowned. Sioux Indians killed half of the 150 who reached the Mississippi's west bank. Only about 150 of Black Hawk's 1,000 people survived. The tragedy was that, despite the Indians' repeated surrender attempts that the soldiers did not understand, extermination occurred without regard for age, sex, or common humanity.

Once the war was over, everything changed. Southern Wisconsin land sold for $1.25 an acre in the 1830s. My great-grandfather, Andreas Boltz, left Germany for America to escape universal conscription to the army. Immigrants came from Finland, Sweden, Denmark, and the other nations of Europe, hoping for a better life for themselves and their children. The first settlers found the Rock River clean, clear, and drinkable. Within one generation, however, every rain left the river running brown with its watershed's soils. Lake Koshkonong's outlet was dammed to deepen its water level. Wild rice was flooded, with the remnants grubbed out by carp introduced from Europe. Elk, deer, bison, and wolves were killed until none were left.

We look back and see what can only be described with a hard word: *ecocide*. To that painful term must be added another, *genocide*, for the original inhabitants were pushed out, killed, and replaced. My home, the city that fed, educated, and prepared me to be a Christian minister, Fort Atkinson, was built on a bloody foundation!

In 2020 my son Martin drove his van across America, a few weeks after Tonya died, stopping at places that Tonya and he had always wanted to visit. My brother John suggested that since Tonya often said she was an Owens, perhaps he could take some of her ashes to Fort Atkinson, where our parents and grandparents are buried. When I returned from an afternoon walk, on my computer was a picture Martin sent of the Owens's tombstone, where my dad and mother are buried. Then I heard my brother John and Martin offer a simple burial ceremony, as Martin scattered some of her remains over the graves. Ashes of beloved Black and white family members are now mingled together.

As I read how the white settlers plowed the land and planted crops on Sauk mothers', fathers', grandparents', and children's graves, I thought about how I would feel if conquerors did that to Mother's grave, blew up the Civil War monuments, and planted corn! The Fort Atkinson in which I was born and reared was a testimony to what progressive citizens can do when working together for the mutual good. If aliens invaded, killed, conquered, and sought to replace us with their history, religion, agriculture, and institutions, how much they would lose as all we learned and built would be plowed. Correspondingly, I wondered how much we European-origin "white" folks lost when we killed the Sauks and took their land!

Hugh Highsmith wrestled with these realities:

> There is little question that Indian treatment by whites was destructive. We can wish that some means might have been found to make a transition to a government dominated by or shared with whites, but the end of life as Indians knew it surely could never have been much in doubt. Consider that, on the basis of estimated early Indian populations in Wisconsin, an average county supported only a few hundred Indians. To the whites the country appeared to be empty and unused. Today in Jefferson County, 68,500 or more people live on this land and produce food for another 100,000. To believe that Indian culture as it existed in 1800 could have been isolated from the rest of

> the world is unrealistic. Progress—if that is what it is—is ruthless.[2]

Evils we tolerate or visit on others come home to haunt us. Shortly before he died in 1996, my parents' friend Norman Wittlief told me how Wisconsin had changed since he was a boy. After the Sauk and other native peoples of Wisconsin were pushed out and killed, hardworking settlers created small farms that produced most of their own food. To earn money, farmers separated cream from whey, fed the whey to the pigs, and hauled the cans of cream by horse-drawn wagon to a creamery where it was made into butter and cheese. As he grew older, Norman witnessed many changes. Motorized transportation allowed centralized creameries to be built in Fort Atkinson. Milk no longer had to be hauled to market but was picked up from the farm. Putting milk in spring water, which had no cash outlay, was no longer deemed adequate by health authorities. Rural electrification made refrigeration of milk possible so it could be picked up. Milk production costs increased. What people in the cities bought, as well as the standards they imposed, determined what happened to farmers and their land.

During Norman Wittlief's life, most farmers owned their land. Today corporate farms dominate the landscape. The application of industrial processes to farming made it difficult for small farmers to survive. Large dairy plants in large cities bought out and replaced small independent creameries. Children who grew up on farms and in small towns left home and followed jobs to the cities. Slowly, Thomas Jefferson's dream of an America peopled by independent farmers died as wealth and economic decision-making became concentrated in fewer and fewer hands.

Doing a Fearless, Searching Moral Inventory

How do people change for the better—how does homeland healing happen? In Alcoholics Anonymous and Al-Anon, we turn control of our lives over to God as we understand God. When we do a moral inventory of ourselves, we build on our strengths and gifts, as well as identify ways we injured others, and make amends. When a person gets ill, the first step to healing is letting go and letting a loving God take control. Diagnosing the sickness is the next step, for until an accurate diagnosis, we have no idea what course of treatment to follow. Likewise, I cannot ignore the blood-stained ground on which my town was built, but instead must examine what happened, much like a trained physician studies symptoms.

When I returned to my hometown and started asking myself how homeland healing could happen, I started out with unformed opinions, drawing on observations, experiences, and cultural traditions shaped during my lifetime (often in unaware ways). I learned the Golden Rule in the First Methodist Church of Fort Atkinson: "Do unto others as you would have them do unto you." I also decided after accepting Jesus Christ as Lord and Savior that I would follow his teachings. "You shall love the Lord your God with all your heart and with all your soul and with all your mind," he directed, and "You shall love your neighbor as yourself" (Matthew 22:37, 39). Jesus promised that when we followed him and obeyed God's commandments, we would live, now and forever. Moreover, the Holy Spirit would pour out blessings of love, joy, patience, and peace (Galatians 5:22).

When I consider the massacre of the Sauks through the lens of God's commandments, I see a consistent pattern. Euro-Americans had no intention of treating Sauks as neighbors. They were disinterested in their own well-being. For them, Indigenous people were like wolves who must be killed or pushed out so that civilized, English-speaking people could replace them. In other words, expanding Euro-American civilization was more important than Jesus Christ and God's commandments.[3] Churches restricted applying the love of God and neighbor, therefore, only to "civilized" people. Evangelism, indeed, shaped the conversion of Native American people to Jesus Christ in a way that also meant converting them to American civilization, expressed in the nineteenth-century missionary slogan, "Kill the Indian, not the man!" When the Golden Rule is broken and there is no repentance, like cancer, destructive behavior grows. What happened in Wisconsin in 1832 was only one instance of the conquest of US and Canadian Indigenous peoples, for ecocide and genocide are symptoms of the pernicious illness diagnosed by Alexander Humboldt.

Part of the diagnosis of the cause of our impending social and ecological crisis, therefore, is that Euro-American civilization was confused with God, and religion was limited so that it supported and even carried this idolatry.[4]

Many years ago, American Indian Movement (AIM) leader Russell Means told a story about breaking down God's creation that I have never forgotten.[5] God created the earth—round, the sun—round, the moon—round. God created all the creatures: the badger, buffalo, wolf, snake. God made the two-leggeds also. Native Americans knew they differed from the animals, but they looked around and saw that the creatures' lives were circles: birth—life—death—new birth. Even a tree teaches the lesson of circles, as season follows season. Understanding what they saw, Indigenous peoples sought to fit themselves into the circles and lived with respect for all their relatives: Mother Earth, sister and brother creatures, sun and moon.

The white man came to America and called the forest "wilderness" and the creatures "wild." Since Native peoples lived in what he called wilderness, he thought of them as wild, too, savages either to be assimilated into white, European ways or eliminated. Through reason, he saw a movement from the past through the present into the future in a straight line, and he destroyed every creature that seemed to stand in the way of "progress." Thus, the white man failed to fit into the round way of life. Means observed that it was because we were blinded from using our reason to hear, see, and act accordingly.

My Navajo colleague Rev. John Coy Cook, tells a Coyote story about what happens when we break God's family apart. Bright, inquisitive, always running around looking for something to eat, Coyote seems much like we modern Americans. When his appetite becomes unlimited, however, his greed drives him to cross natural and social boundaries that stand in his way, as did the bankers and stockbrokers who precipitated the stock market's collapse.

Imaginative, strong, and always hungry, Coyote gets bright ideas and plunges into action. He does not care about what the consequences will be and ends up messing up the lives of others and hurting himself. Unlimited greed and violence sickens everyone. Coyote, who is such a curious animal, observed the birds flying. He wanted to be better, to fly. The more he thought about it, the more he asked the birds, "How come you can fly? How do you do it? Tell me your secrets!"

The birds replied, "We are birds. We are supposed to fly. You are Coyote. You are not supposed to fly. Creator made you a coyote. Your purpose is to live out who you are."

But Coyote did not change. He continued his "scientific" investigations, stepping outside normal predator-prey relationships.[6] He tried to force the birds to consider matters and bestow on him something they were not able to do. He wanted to have them declare him a bird. He was looking for secrets and saw great benefits in being able to fly. Imagine who he could catch and how much he could eat if he could fly like the hawks and the eagles!

Coyote's probing into their lives, habits, and secrets finally frustrated and angered the birds. They held a council meeting and decided they needed to do something drastic. The hawks came diving down and shot Coyote with feathered arrows, and he died.

Every human being is created in God's image, and the Lord loves every one of us. All living creatures belong to one family—when one advances, we all benefit; when one is hurt, we all suffer. There will be liberty and justice for all—or for none! Decades of growth and development have put us way out of balance with the natural order. Bad times follow good ones. Lean years come after fat ones. The Bible, however, rings with a message of hope.

Time of Turning

God speaks so that we may hear and do the Word. Biblical faith has much to say about hearing God's Word to seek liberty and justice for all and turning from destructive ways to life-giving ones. Listening precedes action for the good of all. When we fail to listen and learn, we repeat the past's destructive acts. Human beings are speaking creatures. Listening implies respect, which is the first step to a positive relationship with God, nature, and other human beings. Listening, of course, does not imply accepting all the ideas shared, nor commitment to the perspective from which thoughts arise. Instead, listening implies the willingness to seek to understand both thoughts and perspectives from the viewpoint of the speaker. Dialogue emerges when listening and speaking become reciprocal.

Greed prevents communication, as when the understanding of Native Americans was pursued only to gain their land. Cortez and Miles Standish never got to know who it was they conquered! Likewise, white slave traders never knew those whom they condemned to death on the journey over the ocean or to back-breaking labor.

Another communication block is found in historic thought disciplines formed by the dominant group's experiences, which force others to translate their understandings into the conquering culture's concepts. Without openness to experiences or differing understandings, arrogance results. One "understands" another without really taking the other person into account.

"We Talk—You Listen!" This slogan of the American Indian Movement in the 1970s and '80s expresses a fundamental truth.

Respectful communication births a new community. Whereas conquerors speak and force those left alive to listen, free people speak and listen to each other. White Euro-Americans approached Indigenous peoples with concepts of eminent domain, colonialism, evangelical and commercial conversion, and oppression. Seeking privileges for themselves, they did not respect the various native cultures, languages, values, and rights. According to the Bible, the Heavenly Listener is the first to hear the cries of the oppressed and come down, speak to them, and free them from slavery (Exodus 3:7-8). Insensitive leaders, like the pharaoh of Egypt, are forced to listen and finally to do justice, even against their will.

Many of our ancestors left family and homeland to come to a land of opportunity, promising liberty and justice for all. An empty dream? Not according to the First Commandment: "I am the LORD your God, who brought you out of the land of Egypt, out of the house of slavery; you shall have no other gods before me" (Exodus 20:2). The Bible says the universe's Creator hears the cries of oppressed slaves and delivers them from bondage.

Every immigrant who came to our land had a struggle to make it. We white people are here because of the labor and sacrifices of those who succeeded and were able to buy a house and a car and save a little for the future. Is it any wonder we try to show we are somebody by what we buy and consume? My father started out with little, was out of work during the Depression, and then got a loan from my mother's parents to buy a general store in Cambria, Wisconsin. He was very proud that he earned enough to pay off the loan, send my brother and me to college, and provide for himself and Mother in their old age.

John Winthrop wrote as he sailed across the ocean with the Pilgrims that America's divine calling was to be the light of the world, a city on a hill. With all our failings, the United States has often indeed been a light to the nations, a place where hardworking immigrants could pursue liberty and justice and happiness, a place built by the labors of people of many skin colors, a place where a revolution and then a civil war were fought so liberty and justice could be, indeed, for all.

Yet evil persists. After opening the door to a new day in race relations in the United States, Dr. Martin Luther King Jr. was murdered. Decades later people are still harassed and killed because of the color of their skin. And each year many plant and animal species become extinct due to human activity.

America now stands before the Judge. Alexander Humboldt pressed President Thomas Jefferson—who inspired the Bill of Rights—to act on his convictions, stop taking land from Indigenous peoples, end slavery, and stop the destruction of ecosystems by the plantation economy. Jefferson, however, chose to make American expansion his priority, leaving a divisive legacy down to the present.

Our Protestant ancestors, however, have a word for us about living in the light of God, and I imagine it to say:

> We heard about a land of liberty and justice where we could pursue happiness. We left everything to come to America. We learned English, sacrificed, worked hard, and made a better life for our children. We made and kept treaties with the Lenape people, and we sought to establish a peaceable kingdom in Penn's Woods. We fought to free our colonies from British domination and helped unite our separate colonies into a democratic United States of America. We sent preachers to the frontiers and missionaries to other lands who proclaimed Jesus Christ as Lord and Savior, baptized believers, formed self-governing congregations, and started colleges, universities, and hospitals.

I might also hear other ancestors speak words of hope:

> After more than a thousand years of discrimination, persecution, and pogroms, we Jews emigrated to a land where by law we were guaranteed freedom to worship as we chose—we built synagogues, hospitals, social welfare institutions, and worked for liberty and justice for all.
>
> Though a Protestant culture treated us as non-Christians, we Roman Catholics kept and deepened our faith, built churches, schools, and hospitals, not only lifting up our people but also those of other faiths.

Those who went before us did not sit by and let greedy exploitation of people and land destroy the promise of a democracy organized of, by, and for the people. I can picture them saying:

> We held on to our tribal languages and traditional ways, struggled to get our treaty rights honored, and told you to care for the land, water, and all our animal and bird relatives. We fought and died in the Civil War to hold the union together and end slavery. We organized schools to educate freedmen and welcomed white women from the North who came to help us. We formed trade unions and organized voluntary associations to reform the country so everyone could be free and equal. We started soil and water conservation movements, established national parks, and passed fish and game laws to protect wildlife. We formed the women's suffrage movement and finally got the right to vote. We fought World War II against totalitarian dictators to make the world safe for democracy. We marched for our civil rights and saw an African American elected president.

> "Your words give us hope, Dad and Mom, Grandma and Grandpa," say our children, "but the progress and development you depended upon and expanded over the whole planet poured so much carbon into the air that climate change threatens us with floods, droughts, and drastic variability in weather patterns." Forests are still being logged and burned. Every day more living beings are going extinct. For a long time, Americans ignored what was happening, as when blights and insects from other lands killed our forests of chestnut, elm, hemlock, and ash trees. We did nothing when cave explorers brought back from Europe a deadly disease that killed millions of bats. The country elected politicians who suggest America can be first if we beat down people who are trying to climb up from the bottom of the well and do more of what made us rich and prosperous in the past. Then we were surprised when COVID came to America. Now when we see what's going on, we feel like giving up in despair!

In my inner being, I can hear those who have gone before reply:

> So you face human-caused climate change that has resulted in droughts and floods. So you cannot keep on with unlimited expansion of industries, cities, and population. So you are beginning to see why Native Americans have been saying we have to get in balance with nature. So days of comfortable, easy living are over. So a few super-rich people control most of the wealth, leaving people struggling to earn a living.
>
> So what's new? Our lives weren't easy, but we left a world for you with many opportunities. So the old sins of conquering nature and people to feed human greed, vainglory, and power—"me, mine, ours"—are taking you

> down. That's why in the early days of America we had national days of repentance to turn from ways that hurt ourselves and others back to a just, loving God whom we asked to forgive and guide us in doing justice, loving kindness, and walking humbly with the LORD. As words of hate rise from talk shows and tweets, perhaps you can listen to the psalmist: "Search me, O God, and know my heart; test me and know my thoughts. See if there is any wicked [Heb. 'hurtful'] way in me, and lead me in the way everlasting." (Psalm 139:23-24)

You belong to a divinely inspired, caring community that transcends whatever divides and destroys creatures. Jesus called it the kingdom of God. Paul pointed to the righteousness of God. The prophets foresaw *shalom*, God's peace, when ecological wholeness and social justice will join as wolf and lamb lie down together and a little child leads them (Isaiah 11:6). I was privileged to know the late Reaves Nahwooks, a Comanche theologian who showed me that being at peace includes relationships between self and God, self and other people, and between self and nature:

> All relationships tie together to God. When you are in proper relationship, that is perfection. God lures toward a better world with each decision. Hope for the better is always there. God gives us decisions. Those options are there for us to make. When we fall short, that is sin. We must consider the whole, everything, because everything is related. When we come close to peace, it results in balance and harmony.[7]

Business tycoon Donald Trump, Reaves used to say, was commonly thought to be successful because of his money and power. In much of modern-day America, we omit, however, whether

Trump is at peace with himself, with others, and with nature. When Indigenous people hear the word *power*, they think of healing and medicine. The Comanche and Cherokee languages have no word that says "success" is the goal of life. Instead, peace and proper relationships are the goal.

"From a Native American Indian point of view, integrity of creation has to be first," Nahwooks said. "Creation is continually going on. The natural order is the ground of all life. Next comes the theme of peace, since it expresses the balance and harmony of all relationships. Justice logically follows, with its focus on righting oppression."[8] Nahwooks demonstrated how Indian thought helps us see life as a cycle, which is tied to the coexistence of opposites and polarities. When one overwhelms another, the opposite force brings life back into balance again.

A powerful biblical image pictures the people of God as the body of Christ, one body with many members (1 Corinthians 12). You and I are related to all living beings and to the earth:

- *We belong to one human family.* Though skin color, cultural origin, language, and nationality differ, humans have a common origin and a common destiny. There is one body with many members.
- *We belong to an animal family.* Blood, bones, flesh, and brain speak of a common biological heritage. Our bodies are made of the dust of the earth and the salt of the sea. We rejoice on good days and suffer when we are hurt. Wolves and whales, birds and humans belong to the family of living creatures. One body, many members.
- *We belong to ecological families.* We are part of immense living systems that sustain themselves from generation to generation. Changes occur, responses are made, and life goes on. Summer and winter, spring and fall, we belong to the seasons. Birth, growth, aging, death, new birth—we belong to the generations. Earth and sea, air and water, the great water cycle—we are a part. One body, many members.

■ *We belong to an economic family.* We eat, drink, and are satisfied. When there is not enough, we thirst and starve and suffer. The flesh and fiber of other lives sustain us. We modify our environment in our struggle to live and make a living. One body, many members.

■ *We belong to a spiritual family.* At their best, religions and cultures point beyond themselves to an ultimate source of being. We recognize that our own wisdom, ethics, and practice of worship are far from the ultimate, and see that what is best in human life is grounded in the deepest reality. We are not aliens on a tiny planet wandering through a vast universe but are citizens of a heavenly kingdom. One body, many members.

■ *We belong to a North American family.* All who live on this continent share common experiences and fates. The various colors, faintly imprinted in our skins and reflected in a vast array of different hues, remind us of the pain in our past relationships and point to the possibility of a new future. Land and water still sustain life. Forests still breathe in carbon dioxide and give off oxygen. The sun still shines. Animals still abide in the wilderness, and domestic beasts and pets depend on us for their care. Those dwelling here on this continent belong to North America. One body, many members.

Around the lake and on the banks of the Rock River, the Indigenous people built mounds in conical, animal, and linear shapes. Archaeological studies show that some of these mounds were shaped 2,500 years ago. A great deal of labor, time, and design tradition went into their construction. Modern artists think of animal, bird, and linear mounds as abstract earth sculptures, which must have been carefully planned and measured before they were built.

In 1836 Fort Atkinson had twenty-five to thirty-five mounds, with another dozen just to the city's north. Today only one earthen structure survives within city limits: the Panther Intaglio. Some disappeared when the fields were plowed. Others were used for fill dirt.

> Pioneer life was hard. The mounds were, as Rankin mentions, "in the way." The Indians whose ancestors built them were not—at the time—well respected by the settlers and seemed to know nothing about the mounds or even to be interested in them. The sculptured piles of dirt were easy to level or use as fill, and unfortunately, the early settlers did just that. Future residents continued to destroy the mounds until 1987 when Indian burial mounds came under the protection of Wisconsin's burial site legislation.[9]

Why were the mounds created? The purpose of the animal, bird, and linear earthen structures, which ranged from one hundred to five hundred feet long, is not clear, but R. Clark Mallam of Luther College said,

> I think it is possible that the mounds in all their varied forms expressed metaphorically the relationships among humans that were absolutely essential for the perpetuation of this particular lifeway. What the mounds symbolize is balance and harmony—idealized natural and cyclical regularity—and the forces of life which were critical to production. If this proposition is anywhere near correct, the forces above the earth were represented by birds, the forces on earth were represented by bears and other forms, while water, the sustaining and necessary element for life, is manifest in the forms of "lizards, turtles, etc." The idealized harmony they selectively noted in the natural world was synonymous with the harmonious social relationships that needed to be actualized in their lifeway.[10]

Since we belong to all families of God's creation, we can reenter community and be healed, get in tune with life as the Creator made it. For the Navajo people, the Coyote story does not end with him dead on the ground. After a while, Horned Toad found him and said, "Poor guy, he didn't know what he was doing. He should not be dead." Horned Toad called in the plant people, the bird people, and all the animal people. They held a council and decided to let Coyote live again. Water, plants, and the environment pitched in to help the arrogant one, finally introduced by his own behavior to suffering and death. A healing ceremony began. They brought him back to life to be a good coyote.[11]

Historian Highsmith sees a way out of the ecology-justice crises that threaten to destroy us. He listened to the silent voices of those who had gone before throughout his life, studied the composition and structure of the mounds, and wrote with delight about their beautiful forms. With persistence, Highsmith learned much from archaeological findings about the lives of those who made the mounds. He mourns the destruction of so many mounds. More than this, he has not only spent his own money to preserve the remaining mounds but also became active to get the county to save the structures in a special park.

As I read Highsmith, I wondered if perhaps these ancient creations might have something to teach us if we put our ears to the ground from which we have come and to which we will soon return. If we stand with respect near the Panther Intaglio, it is as if voices are speaking: "We once walked this land. Listen, listen to our silent voices!"

Respect and appreciation for those who went before us are necessary if we are to learn. We not only have the mounds but also the land the Native Americans passed on to our care. Though Koshkonong was polluted and degraded by progress, the lake, the river, and the land remain. If we show respectful restraint to our Indian ancestors, the place will restore itself to live into its name, "the one who feeds us." The ancient people created physical expressions of what they saw, lived from, and valued. The mounds express beauty, balance, blessing. This must have been the deep, central purpose of their civilization, just as contemporary industrial civilization's purpose is unlimited growth to make money.

> But this victory (of the Spanish over the Aztecs) from which we all derive, Europeans and Americans both, delivers as well a terrible blow to our capacity to feel in harmony with the world, to belong to a pre-established order. Its effect is to repress human communication with the world, to produce the illusion that all community is inter-human community. What was done in the colonies came home to the center of Western European civilization in World Wars I and II.[12]

Through their earth sculptures, the ancient ones are speaking to us. Like Hugh Highsmith, let us put our ears to the ground.[13] Maybe an angel who lived long ago will speak:

> This we know. We are not dead. We know the One who made us, even as the Great Mystery made you who for a brief time walk upright on the land. Look at the Panther we left traced in the ground and consider your animal relatives. See the Turtle and remember the water foundations of the planet. Concentrate on the Bird and think of health-giving air. Do what your Bible teaches. Cease to do evil, learn to do good. Undo what wrongs you can. Return land to the Winnebago, Sauk, Chippewa and let them take care of it in traditional ways. Listen to what they have to say to you. Turn from ways of death to life. Then you shall live and be happy and your descendants will speak well of you.

Conclusion

The Bible has many ways of speaking about leaving home and getting lost. Jesus tells us that God is like a poor woman who lost a coin and looked everywhere until she found it (Luke 15:8-10). In the adjoining parable, God is like a father whose youngest son took his inheritance, went to a far country, and lived like a "Once-ler" until he used up every cent (Luke 15:11-24). Hard times came. As the son was starving, he came to himself and started home. Every day, his dad watched the road, hoping to see his son. One day, way down the road, he saw his boy coming home. Before the son got to the door, the father ran out and threw his arms around his son. The son had gone over and over what he would say: "Father, I have sinned against heaven and before you; I am no longer worthy to be called your son" (verses 18-19). But his father threw the best robe in the house over his son's shoulders and started a big celebration. "For this son of mine was dead and is alive again; he was lost and is found!" (verse 24).

It is called self-righteousness, injustice, hypocrisy, pride, sin, breaking the commandments, and worshipping the creation rather than the Creator. Story after story, life after life, warns us to stop being "Once-lers" and go back home. Along with the warnings goes a deep affirmation. We "coyotes of the world" can leave arrogance behind and allow ourselves to be ministered to and healed. We can go home.

Notes

1. Hugh Highsmith, *The Mounds of Koshkonong and the Rock River* (Fort Atkinson Historical Society, 1997), 52.

2. Highsmith, *The Mounds of Koshkonong and the Rock River*, 51.

3. When Columbus landed on what is now Haiti and the Dominican Republic, he called it heaven on earth. Perhaps a million and a half Indigenous people lived peaceably. Twenty years later, only ten thousand "Indians" clung to a wretched existence as slaves of the Spanish conquerors. Christian religion was imposed by force of arms. The natural environment was exploited to make plantations. Genocide and ecocide went together.

4. See George Tinker, *Missionary Conquest* (Fortress, 1993); Luis N. Rivera, *A Violent Evangelism: The Political and Religious Conquest of the Americas* (Westminster John Knox, 1992).

5. Author's recall of presentation by Russell Means, First Methodist Church, Germantown, Philadelphia, 1972.

6. John C. Cook and Owen D. Owens, *Healing the Coyote in Me: The Navajo Coyoteway Blessing Ceremony*, audiobook (Leave a Little Room Foundation, 2008).

7. Author conversation with Reaves Nahwooks, March 1990.

8. Author conversation with Reaves Nahwooks. Distinguished Catholic theologian Walter Burghardt said that the biblical idea of justice can be defined as fidelity to the demands of a relationship—king with people, judge with complainants, family with tribe and kinfolk, the community with the resident alien and suffering in their midst, and all people with the covenant with God. Justice was a whole network of relationships, Burghardt said, and the most profound basis of these relationships was Israel's covenant with God. God is just, defending or vindicating God's people, punishing violations of the covenant, and keeping divine promises. People are just when we are in right relationship with God, with other humans, and with the earth. *Long Have I Loved You: A Theologian Reflects on His Church* (Orbis, 2000), 166.

9. Highsmith, *The Mounds of Koshkonong and the Rock River*, 115.

10. R. Clark Mallam, *Wisconsin Archeologist*, September 1980, quoted in Highsmith, *The Mounds of Koshkonong and the Rock River*, 111.

11. Karl W. Luckert, *Coyoteway: A Navajo Holyway Healing Ceremonial*, Johnny C. Cooke, Navajo interpreter (University of Arizona Press and Museum of Northern Arizona Press, 1979), 22. "Coyote does not remain the epitome of evil; rather, he becomes the prototype of all subsequent Coyoteway patients and healers. According to the ancient way of Coyote, all subsequent sufferers—though they may have brought their suffering upon themselves through 'Coyoteeing around'—are given a chance for recovery. Divine grace and participation abounds over merit" (22).

12. Tzvetan Todorov, *The Conquest of Mexico* (Oxford University Press, 1999), 97.

13. See David Graeber and David Wengrow, *The Dawn of Everything: A New History of Humanity* (Farrar, Straus and Giroux, 2021), 37–46, who show how Europeans learned from the tribes in North America, who lived in generally free societies. "When it came to the questions of personal freedom, equality of men and women, sexual mores, or popular sovereignty, or even theories of depth psychology, indigenous American attitudes are likely to be far closer to the reader's own than seventeenth-century European ones."

About the Author

Throughout his life, Owen D. Owens was active in congregational life, mission, and environmental conservation. For over 50 years, he was committed to learning how God is leading us to a future of ecological wholeness and social justice, where the Biblical hope of peace on earth will become a daily reality.

Owens co-chaired the Religious Campaign for Creation Care with Rabbi Warren Stone. He co-founded the Valley Forge Chapter of Trout Unlimited and chaired the National Council of Churches of Christ's Eco-Justice Work Group. An ordained Methodist minister, Owens served American Baptists in their home mission work from 1968 to 2000, researching and planning programs, evangelism, church renewal, ecology, and racial justice.

He served on Rev. Jitsuo Morikawa's evangelism staff from 1968 to 1976, where the connections of ecology to justice emerged from a four-year strategic planning process by the Board and staff of the American Baptist Home Mission Societies. Active in prayer movements for many years, with the Church and Community Development staff under the direction of Dr. Ernestine Galloway, he organized the 1984 Baptist Prayer Conference which brought together more than 500 leaders from Baptist Indian and other racial/ethnic groups and Euro-Americans, following up this event with more than a decade of summer prayer conferences at the ABC Green Lake Conference Center.

He was a planning consultant to the Baptist Indian Caucus from 1979 to 1989, helped create the Seeds of Renewal Program for Small-Sized ABC Churches, chaired the Valley Creek Restoration Partnership, and assisted in starting the FRAC Action Coalition of

Southeast Pennsylvania (organized in 2010 to seek effective regulation of Marcellus Shale gas drilling). He wrote *American Baptist Evangelistic Life Style* and church renewal resources. He also co-authored *Healing the Coyote in Me: The Navajo Coyoteway Blessing Ceremony* (Denver, CO: Leave a Little Room Foundation, 2008) with the Rev. John Coy Cook (a member of the Navajo Nation). His other books included *Spiritual Help in Hard Times: The Bible's Hope for Life on Earth* (Santa Rosa, CA: Religious Campaign for Creation Care, 2016), *Living Waters: How to Save Your Local Stream* (Rutgers University Press, 1993), *Growing Churches for a New Age* (Valley Forge: Judson Press, 1980), and *Stones into Bread* (Valley Forge: Judson Press, 1976).

Owens studied the Sociology of Religion, earning his PhD from the University of California, Berkeley, and the Graduate Theological Union. He also attended the Union Theological Seminary in New York City, earning a Bachelor of Divinity. He also studied at Northwestern University and earned an MA. He also graduated with a BA from Beloit College.